Vocabulary

Elizabeth Chesla

LearningExpress®

NEW YORK

Library of Congress Cataloging-in-Publication Data:
Chesla, Elizabeth L.
 Just in time vocabulary / Elizabeth Chesla.—1st ed.
    p. cm.
 ISBN 1-57865-507-4 (pbk.)
 1. Vocabulary—Study and teaching. I. Title.
 LB1574.5.C44 2004
 372.44—dc22

                                    2003019051

Printed in the United States of America
9 8 7 6 5 4 3 2 1
First Edition

ISBN 1-57685-507-4

For more information or to place an order, contact LearningExpress at:
    55 Broadway
    8th Floor
    New York, NY 10006

Or visit us at:
    www.learnatest.com

ABOUT THE AUTHOR

Elizabeth Chesla is the author of *501 Vocabulary Questions*, *TOEFL Exam Success*, *Reading Comprehension Success*, *Write Better Essays*, and contributing author of *GMAT Exam Success*, *ACT Exam Success*, *GED Exam Success*, and many other writing and reading guides and test-preparation books. She teaches English language arts at Seton Hall University and lives in South Orange, New Jersey.

CONTENTS

Introduction

You are just a few weeks—perhaps even just a few days—from taking a big exam that will test your vocabulary, and you haven't begun to study. Perhaps you just haven't had the time; after all, your schedule is filled with work, family, and other obligations. Or perhaps you have had the time, but you have procrastinated; vocabulary has never been your strong suit. Maybe you have waited until the last minute because you simply need a refresher course, not an exhaustive review. Or maybe you didn't even realize that your test included a section on vocabulary, and now you have only a short time to prepare.

If any of these scenarios sound familiar, then *Just in Time Vocabulary* is the right book for you. Designed specifically for last-minute test preparation, *Just in Time Vocabulary* is a fast, accurate way to build your essential vocabulary skills. With over 350 commonly tested words, this workbook will help you review the vocabulary words and skills you already know and teach you other words and strategies that you will need for the exam. In just ten short chapters, you will get just the essentials, just in time for passing your big test.

THE *JUST IN TIME* TEST-PREP APPROACH

At LearningExpress, we know how important test scores and an educated vocabulary can be. Whether you are preparing for the PSAT, SAT, GRE, GMAT, or a Civil Service exam, or you simply need to improve your fundamental vocabulary skills *fast*, our *Just in Time* streamlined approach can work for you. Each skill-building lesson includes:

- 35–40 commonly tested vocabulary words
- a brief Benchmark Quiz to help you assess your knowledge of the words and skills in the chapter
- a brief lesson covering an essential vocabulary skill and word definitions
- specific tips and strategies to use as you study and during the exam
- a 25-question practice quiz followed by detailed answers and explanations to help you measure your progress

Our *Just in Time* series also includes the following features:

-  *Extra Help* sidebars that refer you to other Learning-Express skill builders or other resources that can help you learn more about a particular topic

-  *Glossary* sidebars with key definitions

- *Rule Book* sidebars highlighting the rules that you absolutely need to know

- *Shortcut* sidebars with tips for reducing your study time—without sacrificing accuracy

- *Cheat Sheet* sidebars with tips and rules-of-thumb for last-minute test preparation

- *A Complete Vocabulary List* of all the words in each chapter

- A *Pronunciation Key* to reference as needed

No vocabulary book can cover all of the words you *might* come across on a standardized test, and here we have limited our list to just over 350 words. But this book is not just about building your word base; it is also about building those essential skills that can help you determine the meaning of words you don't know. The vocabulary words in this book have been carefully chosen to reflect not only what you are likely to see on an exam, but also what you are likely to come across regularly in books, newspapers, lectures, and other daily activities.

HOW TO USE THIS BOOK

The ten chapters in this book are divided into two sections. Chapters 1–5 present specific study and vocabulary skills while chapters 6–10 are word list chapters. While each chapter can stand on its own as an effective vocabulary skill builder, this book will be most effective if you complete each chapter in order, beginning with Chapter 1, so you can sharpen your study and vocabulary skills before you focus on building your word base.

Here is a brief outline of each chapter:

- **Chapter 1: Study Skills** reviews fundamental study strategies including how to budget your time, create a study plan, and use study aids such as flashcards.
- **Chapter 2: Determining Meaning from Context** reviews how to use context to figure out the meaning of vocabulary words.
- **Chapter 3: Using Prefixes and Suffixes** reviews how to use word beginnings and endings to determine meaning.
- **Chapter 4: Latin Word Roots** reviews common Latin word roots and how to use your knowledge of word roots to determine meaning.
- **Chapter 5: Greek Word Roots** reviews common Greek word roots and how to use them to determine meaning.
- **Chapter 6: Homophones and Other Commonly Confused Words** reviews homophones and frequently confused word pairs such as *incredible* and *incredulous*.
- **Chapter 7: Magnificent Modifiers** reviews 40 essential adjectives.
- **Chapter 8: Versatile Verbs** reviews 35 verbs you are likely to come across on exams as well as in newspapers, books, and other texts.
- **Chapter 9: Foreign Words and Phrases** reviews 35 foreign terms you should know.
- **Chapter 10: $5 Words** reviews 35 words that are less common in everyday usage but that often appear on standardized tests.

Depending upon how much time you have before the exam, review as much as possible. Review the words from each chapter you have completed before you move on to the next. That way, you will continue to reinforce your knowledge of the words you have already covered before you add more words to your vocabulary.

Think positive. Your big test may be just a short while away, but you are taking the steps you need to prepare . . . *just in time*.

Pronunciation Key

a	hat, carry, fact	**ŏ**	office, salmon, advisor
ă	ago, dependable, pedal	**oh**	oak, boat, sew
ah	palm, father	**ohr**	aboard, score, coarse
ahr	car, chart, farm	**oi**	oil, coin, coy
air	bare, scare, fair	**oo**	ooze, noodle, super
aw	ball, walk, draw	**oor**	pour, cure, sure
ay	stage, blame, day	**or**	for, scorn, horse
b	bat, rabbit, crib	**ow**	out, house, how
ch	church, preacher	**p**	pan, paper, pop
d	day, puddle, bed	**r**	rain, marry, dear
e	egg, head, cherry	**s**	sun, listen, rice
ĕ	end, shaken, trickle	**sh**	share, fishing, cash
ee	eat, treat, tree	**t**	tip, mutter, pot
eer	ear, clear, cheer	**th**	three, strengthen, breath
f	fan, stuffy, relief	**_th_**	this, father, breathe
g	go, regular, fog	**u**	cup, come, shut
h	heed, heaven, unhappy	**ŭ**	supper, delicious, measure
hw	whether, nowhere	**ur**	her, turn, worry
i	it, live, middle	**uu**	cook, put, pull
ĭ	stencil, edible	**v**	vail, sliver, live
ī	icy, tire, sky	**w**	want, aware, quaint
j	jug, tragic, hedge	**y**	you, yarn, yesterday
k	kitten, shaken, track	**z**	zebra, hazy, please
l	lost, trolley, toll	**zh**	division, treasure
m	more, summon, slim		
n	no, dinner, man		
ng	sing, finger, frank		
o	odd, fox, trot		

Adapted from the *Oxford American Dictionary*, Heald Colleges Edition (New York: Avon Books, 1980).

JUST IN TIME Vocabulary

Study Skills

If you have left studying for that big test until the last minute, you may be feeling that your only option is to cram. You might be feeling panicky that you will never have enough time to learn what you need to know. But the "Just in Time" solution is exactly that: "just in time." This means that with the help of this book you can use your available time prior to your test effectively. First, to get ready for your test just in time, you need a plan. This chapter will help you put together a study plan that maximizes your time and tailors your learning strategy to your needs and goals.

There are four main factors that you need to consider when creating your study plan: what to study, where to study, when to study, and how to study. When you put these four factors together, you can create a specific plan that will allow you to accomplish more—in less time. If you have three weeks, two weeks, or even one week to get ready, you can create a plan that avoids anxiety-inducing cramming and focuses on real learning by following the simple steps in this chapter.

WHAT TO STUDY

Finding out what you need to study for your test is the first step in creating an effective study plan. You need to have a good measure of your

1

ability in vocabulary. You can accomplish this by looking over the Table of Contents to see what looks familiar to you and by answering the Benchmark Quiz questions starting in the next chapter. You also need to know exactly what is covered on the test you will be taking. Considering both your ability and the test content will tell you what you need to study.

▶ *Establish a Benchmark*

In each chapter you will take a short, ten-question Benchmark Quiz that will help you assess your skills. This may be one of the most important steps in creating your study plan. Because you have limited time, you need to be very efficient in your studies. Once you take a chapter Benchmark Quiz and analyze the results, you will be able to avoid studying the material you already know. This will allow you to focus on those areas that need the most attention.

A Benchmark Quiz is only practice. If you did not do as well as you anticipated you might, do not be alarmed and certainly do not despair. The purpose of the quiz is to help you focus your efforts so that you can *improve*. It is important to carefully analyze your results. Look beyond your score, and consider *why* you answered some questions incorrectly. Some questions to ask yourself when you review your wrong answers:

- Did you get the question wrong because the vocabulary word was totally unfamiliar?
- Was the vocabulary familiar but were you unable to come up with the right answer due to the question context? In this case, when you read the right answer it will often make perfect sense. You might even think, "I knew that!"
- Did you answer incorrectly because you read the question carelessly?
- Did you make another careless mistake? For example, circling choice **a** when you meant to circle choice **b**.

Next, look at the questions you got correct and review how you came up with the right answer. Not all right answers are created equally.

- Did you simply know the right answer?
- Did you make an educated guess? An educated guess might indicate that you have some familiarity with the word, but you probably need at least a quick review of the definition.
- Or did you make a lucky guess? A lucky guess means that you don't know the word and you will need to learn it.

Your performance on the Benchmark Quiz will tell you several important things. First, it will tell you how much you need to study. For example, if you got eight out of ten questions right (not counting lucky guesses), you might only need to brush up on certain vocabulary words. But if you got five out of ten questions wrong, you will need a thorough review of the chapter. Second, it can tell you what you know well, that is which subjects you *don't* need to study. Third, you will determine which category of words you need to study in-depth, and which words you simply need to refresh your knowledge of.

▶ *Targeting Your Test*

For the "Just in Time" test-taker, it is important to focus your study efforts to match what is needed for your test. You don't want to waste your time learning something that will not be covered on your test. There are three important aspects that you should know about your test before developing your study plan:

- What material is covered?
- What is the format of the test? Is it multiple choice? Fill in the blank? Some combination? Or something else?
- What is the level of difficulty?

How can you learn about the test before you take it? For most standardized tests, there are sample tests available. These tests—which have been created to match the test that you will take—are probably the best way to learn what will be covered. If your test is non-standardized, you should ask your instructor specific questions about the upcoming test.

You should also know how your score will affect your goal. For example, if you are taking the SAT exam, and the median verbal score of students accepted at your college of choice is 550, then you should set your sights on achieving a score of 550 or better. Or, if you are taking the New York City Police Officer exam, you know that you need to get a perfect or near-perfect score to get a top slot on the list. Conversely, some exams are pass or fail. In this case, you can focus your efforts simply on achieving a passing score.

▶ *Matching Your Abilities to Your Test*

Now that you understand your strengths and weaknesses and you know what to expect of your test, you need to consider both factors to determine what material you need to study. First, look at the subject area or question type with which you have the most trouble. If you can expect to find questions of this type on your test, then this subject might be your first priority.

But be sure to consider how much of the test, will cover this material. For example, if there will only be a few questions out of a hundred that test your knowledge of a subject that is your weakest area, you might decide not to study this subject area at all. You might be better served by concentrating on solidifying your grasp of the main material covered on the exam.

The important thing to remember is that you want to maximize your time. You don't want to study material that you already know, and you don't want to study material that you don't need to know. You will make the best use of your time if you study the material that you know the least, but that you most need to know.

WHERE TO STUDY

The environment in which you choose to study can have a dramatic impact on how successful your studying is. If you chose to study in a noisy coffee shop at a small table with dim lighting, it may take you two hours to cover the same material you could read in an hour in the quiet of the library. That is an hour that you don't have to lose! However, for some people the noisy coffee shop is the ideal environment. You need to determine what type of study environment works for you.

▶ *Consider Your Options*

Your goal is to find a comfortable, secure place that is free from distractions. The place should also be convenient and conform to your schedule. For example, the library might be ideal in many respects. However, if it takes you an hour to get there and it closes soon after you arrive you are not maximizing your study time.

For many people studying at home is a good solution. Home is always open and you don't waste any time getting there, but it can have drawbacks. If you are trying to fit studying in between family obligations, you might find that working from home offers too many opportunities for distraction. Chores that have piled up, children or younger siblings who need your attention, or television that captures your interest, are just some of things that might interfere with studying at home. Or maybe you have roommates who will draw your attention away from your studies. Studying at home is a good solution if you have a room that you can work in alone and away from any distractions.

If home is not a good environment for quiet study, the library, a reading room, or a coffee shop are places you can consider. Be sure to pick a place that is relatively quiet and which provides enough workspace for your needs.

▶ *Noise*

Everyone has his or her own tolerance for noise. Some people need absolute silence to concentrate, while others will be distracted without some sort of background noise. Classical music can be soothing and might help you relax as you study. If you think you work better with music or the television on, you should be sure that you are not paying attention to what's on in the background. Try reading a chapter or doing some problems in silence, then try the same amount of work with noise. Which noise level allowed you to work the fastest?

▶ *Light*

You will need to have enough light to read comfortably. Light that is too dim will strain your eyes and make you drowsy. Too bright and you will be uncomfortable and tense. Experts suggest that the best light for reading comes from behind and falls over your shoulder. Make sure your light source falls on your book and does not shine in your eyes.

▶ *Comfort*

Your study place should be comfortable and conducive to work. While your bed might be comfortable, studying in bed is probably more conducive to sleep than concentrated learning. You will need a comfortable chair that offers good back support and a work surface—a desk or table—that gives you enough space for your books and other supplies. Ideally, the temperature should be a happy medium between too warm and too cold. A stuffy room will make you sleepy and a cold room is simply uncomfortable. If you are studying outside your home, you may not be able to control the temperature, but you can dress appropriately. For example, bring along an extra sweater if your local library is skimpy with the heat.

▶ *A Little Help*

When you have settled on a place to study, you will need to enlist the help of your family and friends—especially if you are working at home. Be sure they know that when you go to your room and close the door to study, you do want to be disturbed. If your friends all go to the same coffee shop where you plan to study, you will also need to ask them to respect your study place. The cooperation of your family and friends will eliminate one of the greatest potential distractions.

WHEN TO STUDY

Finding the time in your busy schedule may seem like the greatest hurdle in making your "just in time" study plan, but you probably have more time available than you think. It just takes a little planing and some creativity.

▶ Analyze Your Schedule

Your first step in finding time to study is to map out your day-to-day schedule—*in detail*. Mark a piece of paper in fifteen-minute intervals from the time you get up to the time you generally go to bed. Fill in each fifteen-minute interval. For example, if you work from nine to five, do not simply block that time off as unavailable for study. Write down your daily routine at work and see when you might have some time to study. Lunch is an obvious time. But there may be other downtime in your workday when you can squeeze in a short study session.

You will want to set aside a stretch of time when you plan to study in your designated study place. But you can also be creative and find ways to study for short bursts during your normal routine. For example, if you spend an hour at the gym on the stationary bike, you can read while you cycle. Or you can review flashcards on your bus ride. If you drive to work, you could record some study material on a tape or CD. You could also listen to this tape while you walk the dog.

When you look at your schedule closely, you will probably find you have more time than you thought. However, if you still don't have the time you need, you should rethink your routine. Can you ask your significant other to take on a greater share of the household chores for the few weeks you need to get ready for your test? Is there some activity that you can forgo for the next few weeks? If you normally go to the gym six days a week for an hour and a half, cut down to three days a week for forty-five minutes. You will add over six and a half hours to your schedule without completely abandoning your fitness routine. Remember any changes you make to your schedule are short-term and a small sacrifice, once you consider your goal.

▶ Time Strategies

Now that you know when you have time available you need to use that time to the best advantage. You will probably find that you can set aside one block of time during the day during which you will do the bulk of your studying. Use this time to learn new material or take a practice quiz and review your answers. Use the small spurts of time you have found in your schedule to review with flashcards, cheat sheets, and other tools.

Also consider your learning style and body rhythm when you make your schedule. Does it take you some time to get into material? If so, you should build a schedule with longer blocks of time. Do you have a short attention span? Then you will do better with a schedule of several shorter study periods. No matter your style, avoid extremes. Neither very long study sessions nor very short (except for quick reviews) sessions are an efficient use of time. Whether you are a morning person or a night owl, plan to study when you are most energetic and alert.

Make sure your schedule allows for adequate rest and study breaks. Skipping sleep is not a good way to find time in your schedule. Not only will you be tired when you study, you will be sleep deprived by the time of the test. A sleep-deprived test-taker is more likely to make careless mistakes, lose energy and focus, and become stressed-out by the testing environment. If you plan to do most of your studying in one block of time, say four hours, be sure you leave time to take a study break. Experts have shown that students are more likely to retain material if they take some time to digest it. A five- or ten-minute break to stretch your legs or eat a snack will revive you and give your brain time to absorb what you have learned.

HOW TO STUDY

How you study is just as important as how long—especially if your time is limited. You will need to be in a good physical and mental state, and you will need to use the right tools for the job. You will also need to understand your learning style so that you can select the best study method. And, perhaps most important, you will need methods that will help you to remember not to memorize the material. All these techniques—using the right tools and methods—will help you make the most of your study time.

▶ Sleep Well, Eat Right, and Relax

Does your idea of studying hard include images of staying up into the wee hours and living on fast food and caffeine until the big test? Even though it may seem like you are working hard when you study around the clock and put aside good eating habits in order to save time, you are not working efficiently. If you have ever pulled an all-nighter you know that by four in the morning you can find yourself reading the same page several times without understanding a word. Adequate rest and good nutrition will allow you to be focused and energetic so you can get more work done in less time.

Most people need about eight hours of sleep a night. Do not sacrifice sleep in order to make time to study. Hunger can be a distraction, so don't skip meals. Eat three nutritious meals a day, and keep healthy snacks on hand during a long study session. The key word is *healthy*. Sugary snacks might make you feel energized in the short term, but that sugar rush is followed by a crash that will leave you feeling depleted. Caffeine can have a similar effect. A little caffeine—a morning cup of coffee, for example—can give you a boost, but too much caffeine will make you feel jittery and tense. Tension can affect your ability to concentrate.

Being over-caffeinated is not the only potential source of tension. Pre-exam anxiety can also get in the way of effective studying. If your anxiety about the upcoming test is getting the better of you, try these simple relaxation techniques:

Breathe! Sounds simple, and it is. Taking long, deep breaths can drain the tension from your body. Place one hand on your stomach and the other on your chest. Sit up straight. Inhale deeply through your nose and feel your stomach inflate. Your chest should remain still. Exhale slowly through your mouth and feel your stomach deflate. It is the slow exhalation that helps you relax, so make sure you take your time releasing your breath. Pausing during a study session to take three deep breaths is a quick way to clear your mind and body of tension so that you can better focus on your work.

Tense and relax your muscles. You may not even notice it, but as anxiety mounts your muscles tense. You may tense your neck and shoulders, your toes, or your jaw. This tension can interfere with your concentration. Release the tension held in your muscles by purposefully tensing then relaxing each muscle. Work from your toes to your head systematically.

Visualize a soothing place. Taking a break to mentally visit a place that you find relaxing can be reinvigorating. Close your eyes and conjure up the sights, smells, and sounds of your favorite place. Really try to feel like you are there for five uninterrupted minutes and you will return from your mini vacation ready to study.

▶ The Right Tools for the Job

If you follow the steps above, you will have a rested, energized, and relaxed brain—the most important tool you need to prepare for your exam. But there are other tools that you will need to make your study session the most productive. Be sure that you have all the supplies you need on hand before you sit down to study. To help make studying more pleasant, select supplies that you enjoy using. Here is a list of supplies that you will need:

- a notebook or legal pad dedicated to studying for your test
- pens
- pencils

- pencil sharpener
- highlighter
- index or other note cards
- paper clips or sticky note pads for marking pages
- a calendar or personal digital assistant (which you will use to keep track of your study plan)

▶ *Break It Down*

You may be feeling overwhelmed by the amount of material you have to cover in a short time. This seeming mountain of work can generate anxiety and even cause you to procrastinate further. Breaking down the work into manageable chunks will help you plan your studying and motivate you to get started. It will also help you organize the material in your mind. When you begin to see the large topic as smaller units of information that are connected, you will develop a deeper understanding of the subject. You will also use these small chunks of information to build your study plan. This will give you specific tasks to accomplish each day, rather than simply having time set aside to study for the test.

For example, if you have difficulty remembering prefixes, suffixes, and word roots, you could study a different word part on certain days of the week: On Monday, practice prefixes; on Wednesday, work on suffixes; on Friday, try reviewing Latin roots; and so on. "Learn all word parts" might seem like an overwhelming task, but if you divide the work into smaller pieces, you will find that your understanding of prefixes, suffixes, and word roots improves with practice and patience.

▶ *Your Learning Style*

Learning is not the same for everyone. People absorb information in different ways. Understanding how you learn will help you develop the most effective study plan for your learning style. Experts have identified three main types of learners: visual, auditory, and kinesthetic. Most people use a combination of all three learning styles, but one style might be more dominant. Here are some questions that will help you identify your dominant learning style:

1. If you have to remember an unusual word, you most likely
   a. picture the word in your mind.
   b. repeat the word aloud several times.
   c. trace out the letters with your finger.

2. When you meet new people, you remember them mostly by
   a. their actions and mannerisms.
   b. their names (faces are hard to remember).
   c. their faces (names are hard to remember).

3. In class you like to
   a. take notes, even if you don't reread them.
   b. listen intently to every word.
   c. sit up close and watch the instructor.

A visual learner would answer **a**, **c**, and **c**. An auditory learner would answer **b**, **b**, and **b**. A kinesthetic learner would answer **c**, **a**, and **a**.

Visual learners like to read and are often good spellers. When visual learners study, they often benefit from graphic organizers such as charts and graphs. Flashcards often appeal to them and help them learn, especially if they use colored markers, which will help them form images in their minds as they learn words or concepts.

Auditory learners, by contrast, like oral directions and may find written materials confusing or boring. They often talk to themselves and may even whisper aloud when they read. They also like being read aloud to. Auditory learners will benefit from saying things aloud as they study and by making tapes for themselves and listening to them later. Oral repetition is also an important study tool. Making up rhymes or other oral mnemonic devices will also help them study, and they may like to listen to music as they work.

Kinesthetic learners like to stay on the move. They often find it difficult to sit still for a long time and will often tap their feet and gesticulate a lot while speaking. They tend to learn best by doing rather than observing. Kinesthetic learners may want to walk around as they practice what they are learning, because using their bodies helps them remember things. Taking notes is an important way of reinforcing knowledge for the kinesthetic learner, as is making flashcards.

It is important to remember that most people learn in a mixture of styles, although they may have a distinct preference for one style over the others. Determine which is your dominant style, but be open to strategies for all types of learners.

▶ *Remember—Don't Memorize*

You need to use study methods that go beyond rote memorization to genuine comprehension in order to be fully prepared for your test. Using study methods that suit your learning style will help you to *really* learn the material you need to know for the test. One of the most important learning strategies is to be an active reader. Interact with what you are reading by asking questions, making notes, and marking passages instead of simply reading the words on the page. Choose methods of interacting with the text that match your dominant learning style.

- **Ask questions.** When you study a word list, ask questions such as, "What do these words have in common? How are they different?" Asking yourself questions will test your comprehension of the material. You are also putting the information into your own words, which will help you remember what you have learned. This can be especially helpful when you are learning definitions. Putting vocabulary definitions into your own words helps you to understand these processes more clearly.
- **Make notes.** Making notes as you read is another way for you to identify key similarities and differences among words and to put definitions into your own words. Writing down these connections can also help you memorize definitions.
- **Highlight.** Using a highlighter is another way to interact with what you are reading. Be sure you are not just coloring, but highlighting key concepts that you can return to when you review.
- **Read aloud.** Especially for the auditory learner, reading aloud can help aid in comprehension. Hearing words and their definitions read aloud can clarify their meanings for you.
- **Make connections.** Try to relate new vocabulary to words you already know. It might be helpful, for example, to explain to a friend how a pair of synonyms are similar as well as how they slightly differ in meaning or degree.
  Reading actively is probably the most important way to use your study time effectively. If you spend an hour passively reading and retaining little of what you have read, you have wasted that hour. If you take an hour and a half to actively read the same chapter, that is time well spent. However, you will not only be learning new material; you will also need methods to review what you have learned.
- **Flashcards.** Write each word on one side of an index card and its definition, synonyms, and perhaps a sample sentence on the other. Review the flashcards until you can state the meaning of each word without looking at the other side. Just making the cards alone is a way of engaging with the material. You reinforce your knowledge of words and definitions by writing them down. Then, when you have made a stack of cards, you have a portable review system. Flashcards are perfect for studying with a friend and for studying on the go.
- **Mnemonics.** These catchy rhymes, songs, and acronyms are tools that help us remember information. Some familiar mnemonics are "i before e except after c" or ROY G. BIV, which stands for Red Orange

Yellow Green Blue Indigo Violet—the colors of the rainbow. Developing your own mnemonics will help you make a personal connection with vocabulary and help you recall it during your test.

- **Keep a word list.** Write down the meaning of words you come across in your other reading and test preparation. Just writing down the words and their definitions will help seal them in your memory and you will have a great word list to review as you expand your vocabulary.
- **Review, review, review.** Repetition is the key to mastery, especially when it comes to building vocabulary. The more you review the words in this book and on your word list, the sooner you will learn their meanings, and the more comfortable you will be actually using them—which is the key to making them part of your permanent vocabulary.

▶ *Studying with Others*

Studying in a group or with another person can be a great motivator. It can also be a distraction, as it can be easy to wander off the subject at hand and on to more interesting subjects such as last night's game, or some juicy gossip. The key is to choose your study partners well and to have a plan for the study session that will keep you on track.

There are definite advantages to studying with others:

Motivation. If you commit to working with someone else you are more likely to follow through. Also, you may be motivated by some friendly competition.

Solidarity. You can draw encouragement from your fellow test takers and you won't feel alone in your efforts. This companionship can help reduce test anxiety.

Shared expertise. As you learned from your practice questions, you have certain strengths and weaknesses in the subject. If you can find a study partner with the opposite strengths and weaknesses, you can each benefit from your partner's strengths. Not only will you get help, but by offering *your* expertise you will build your confidence for the upcoming test.

There are also some disadvantages to studying with others:

Stress of competition. Some study partners can be overly competitive, always trying to prove that they are better in the subject than you. This can lead to stress and sap your confidence. Be wary of the overly competitive study partner.

Too much fun. If you usually hate studying but really look forward to getting together with your best friend to study, it may be because you spend more time socializing than studying. Sometimes it is better to study with an acquaintance who is well-matched with your study needs and with whom you are more likely to stay on task.

Time and convenience. Organizing a study group can take time. If you are spending a lot of time making phone calls and sending e-mails trying to get your study group together, or if you have to travel a distance to meet up with your study partner, this may not be an efficient strategy.

Weigh the pros and cons of studying with others to decide if this is a good strategy for you.

JUST THE FACTS . . . JUST IN TIME

You have thought about the what, where, when, and how, now you need to put all four factors together to build your study plan. Your study plan should be as detailed and specific as possible. When you have created your study plan, you then need to follow through.

▶ Building a Study Plan

You will need a daily planner, a calendar with space to write, or a personal digital assistant to build your plan. You have already determined the time you have free for study. Now you need to fill in the details. You have also figured out what you need to study, and have broken the material down into smaller chunks. Assign one chunk of material to each of the longer study sessions you have planned. You may need to combine some chunks or add some review sessions depending on the number of long study sessions you have planned in your schedule.

You can also plan how to study in your schedule. For example, you might write for Monday 6:00 P.M. to 9:00 P.M.: Read Chapter 4, make notes, and create set of flashcards. Then for Tuesday 8:30 A.M. to 9:00 A.M. (your commute time), study Chapter 4 flashcards. The key to a successful study plan is to be as detailed as possible.

▶ Staying on Track

Bear in mind that nothing goes exactly as planned. You may need to stay late at work, you may get a nasty cold, soccer practice may go late, or your child might need to go to the doctor. Any number of things can happen to your well-thought-out study plan—and some of them probably will. You will need strategies for coping with life's little surprises.

The most important thing to remember when you get off track is not to panic or throw in the towel. You can adjust your schedule to make up the lost time. You may need to reconsider some of your other commitments and see if you can borrow some time for studying. Or you may need to forego one of your planned review sessions to learn new material. You can always find a few extra minutes here and there for your review.

▶ Minimizing Distractions

There are some distractions, such as getting sick, that are unavoidable. Many others can be minimized. There are the obvious distractions such as socializing, television, and the telephone. There are also less amusing distractions such as anxiety and fear. They can all eat up your time and throw off your study plan. The good news is you can do a lot to keep these distractions at bay.

- **Enlist the help of your friends and family.** Just as you have asked your friends and family to respect your study space, you can also ask them to respect your study time. Make sure they know how important this test is to you. They will then understand that you don't want to be disturbed during study time, and will do what they can to help you stick to your plan.
- **Keep the television off.** If you know that you have the tendency to get pulled into watching TV, don't turn it on even *before* you plan to study. This way you won't be tempted to push back your study time to see how a program ends or see "what's coming up next."
- **Turn off your cell phone and the ringer on your home phone.** This way you won't eat up your study time answering phone calls—even a five-minute call can cause you to lose focus and waste precious time.
- **Use the relaxation techniques discussed earlier** in the chapter if you find yourself becoming anxious while you study. Breathe, tense and relax your muscles, or visualize a soothing place.
- **Banish negative thoughts.** Negative thoughts—such as, "I'll never get through what I planned to study tonight," "I'm so mad all my friends are at the movies and I'm stuck here studying," "Maybe I'll just study for an hour instead of two so I can watch the season finale of my favorite show"—interfere with your ability to study effectively. Sometimes just noticing your negative thoughts is enough to conquer them. Simply answer your negative thought with something positive—"If I study the full two hours, I can watch the tape of my show," "I want to study because I want to do well on the test so I can . . . " and so on.

▶ *Staying Motivated*

You can also get off track because your motivation wanes. You may have built a rock-solid study plan and set aside every evening from 6:00 to 9:00 to study. Then, your favorite team makes it to the playoffs. Your study plan suddenly clashes with a very compelling distraction. Or you may simply be tired from a long day at work or school or from taking care of your family and feel like you don't have the energy for three hours of concentrated study. Here are some strategies to help keep you motivated:

- **Visualization.** Remind yourself of what you will gain from doing well on the test. Take some time to visualize how your life will be positively changed if you accomplish your goal. Do not, however, spend time visualizing how awful your life will be if you fail. Positive visualization is a much more powerful motivator than negative imagery.
- **Rewards.** Rewards for staying on track can be a great motivator, especially for flagging enthusiasm. When you accomplish your study goal, perhaps watch your favorite TV program or have a special treat—whatever it is that will motivate you.
- **Positive feedback.** You can use your study plan to provide positive feedback. As you work toward the test date, look back at your plan and remind yourself of how much you have already accomplished. Your plan will provide a record of your steady progress as you move forward. You can also enlist the help of study partners, family, and friends to help you stay motivated. Let the people in your life know about your study plan and your progress. They are sure to applaud your efforts.

At the end of the day, *you* will be your prime motivator. The fact that you bought this book and have taken the time to create a well-thought out study plan shows that you are committed to your goal. As the slogan says, now all that is left is to "Just do it!" Imagine yourself succeeding on your test and let the excitement of meeting your goal carry you forward.

2

Determining Meaning from Context

In this chapter, you will review one of the most fundamental vocabulary skills: how to use context to determine meaning. Before you begin learning and reviewing context clues, take a few minutes to take this ten-question *Benchmark Quiz*. These questions are similar to the type of questions that you will find on important tests. When you are finished, check the answer key carefully to assess your results. Your Benchmark Quiz analysis will help you determine how much time you need to spend on using context as well as the specific words you need to learn in order to increase your vocabulary power. A complete list of all of the vocabulary words in this lesson is provided at the end of the chapter.

BENCHMARK QUIZ

For each question below, use the context of the sentence to determine the meaning of the italicized word.

1. Make sure the directions are very *explicit* so that no one makes a mistake.

   Explicit means:
   a. intricate, complex.
   b. clearly and fully stated.
   c. chronologically ordered.
   d. ambiguous or implied.
   e. factual, without expressing opinions.

2. The hotel is *teeming* with security personnel because the leaders of several countries are here for a summit meeting.

   To *teem* means:
   a. to close down temporarily.
   b. to lose business due to circumstances beyond one's control.
   c. to be full of, nearly overflowing.
   d. to be under close scrutiny.
   e. to enjoy the benefits of.

3. Karen was relieved to learn that the chemicals in her well water were all *benign*.

   Benign means:
   a. natural.
   b. dangerous.
   c. of local origin.
   d. undisturbed.
   e. harmless.

4. Although it was *futile* because he didn't meet half of the requirements, Jensen applied for the job anyway because it was his dream position.

   Futile means:
   a. useless.
   b. fruitful.
   c. radical.
   d. insane.
   e. stubborn.

5. Although the plot of the film is admittedly *trite*, the characters are so endearing that the movie is highly entertaining despite the old storyline.

   Trite means:
   a. original.
   b. exciting.
   c. complex.
   d. overused.
   e. tragic.

6. Ilka has always *emulated* her older brother, so it is no surprise that she is also pursuing a career as a neuroscientist.

   To *emulate* means:
   a. to support wholeheartedly.
   b. to strive to equal, imitate, or outdo.
   c. to be more successful than.
   d. to regard as inferior.
   e. to feel a strong bond with.

7. Everyone loved Ilona's idea, and she quickly *garnered* enough support for her proposal to present it to the committee.

   To *garner* means:
   a. create.
   b. propose.
   c. demonstrate.
   d. withhold.
   e. gather.

8. Cy's attempt to finally complete the marathon was *thwarted* when he twisted his ankle in the twenty-third mile.

   To *thwart* means:
   a. to injure seriously.
   b. to prevent from accomplishing.
   c. to support actively.
   d. to be excessively competitive.
   e. to set aside a long-awaited goal.

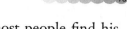

9. Aswad has such a *caustic* sense of humor that most people find his jokes upsetting rather than humorous.

   Caustic means:
   a. bitingly sarcastic.
   b. relentlessly funny.
   c. refreshingly honest.
   d. original, cutting edge.
   e. arrogant, vain.

10. Sandra is truly an *enigma*; although she's lived here for years and everyone knows her, no one seems to know anything about who she is or where she came from.

    An *enigma* is:
    a. a stranger.
    b. an enemy.
    c. a newcomer.
    d. a mystery.
    e. an orphan.

BENCHMARK QUIZ SOLUTIONS

How did you do on identifying context clues? Check your answers here, and then analyze the results to figure out your plan of attack for mastering this topic.

▶ Answers

1. b. *Explicit* means clearly and fully stated; straightforward, exact. The context tells you that the directions need to be clear to prevent an error. If the directions are clearly and fully stated, it will help ensure that no one makes a mistake.

2. c. To *teem* means to be full of, to be present in large numbers. Numerous security personnel typically surround the leader of a country. If there is a meeting of several foreign leaders, there is likely to be a great number of security officers in the hotel.

3. **e.** *Benign* means not harmful or malignant; gentle, mild, having a beneficial effect. Choice **e** is the only answer that makes sense in the context of the sentence; Karen would logically be worried about chemicals in her water and relieved if she learned those chemicals were harmless.

4. **a.** *Futile* means useless, producing no result, hopeless, vain. Jensen's application is useless because he does not meet the minimum requirements for the job.

5. **d.** *Trite* means repeated too often, overly familiar through overuse. The key context clue is the phrase "the old storyline," which indicates that the plot of the movie is overused.

6. **b.** To *emulate* means to try to equal or excel, especially by imitation. The sentence tells you that Ilka is pursuing the same career as her brother, which indicates that she is trying to equal or outdo him through imitation.

7. **e.** To *garner* means to gather, amass, or acquire. The sentence tells you that Ilona quickly found the support she needed to present her idea to the committee; also since the sentence states that people loved Ilona's idea, it is logical to conclude that she would gather their support.

8. **b.** To *thwart* means to prevent the accomplishment or realization of something. Cy's twisted ankle kept him from realizing his attempt to complete the marathon.

9. **a.** *Caustic* means bitingly sarcastic, cutting; able to burn or dissolve by chemical action. The main context clue is that people find Aswad's jokes upsetting rather than humorous; thus choice **a** is the only option that makes sense.

10. **d.** *Enigma* means something that is puzzling or difficult to understand; a baffling problem or riddle. The context tells you that people know who Sandra is, but no one knows anything about her; thus, she remains a mystery.

BENCHMARK QUIZ RESULTS

If you answered 8–10 questions correctly, well done! You are already skilled at determining meaning from context. Give the lesson a quick review and

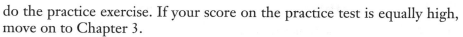

do the practice exercise. If your score on the practice test is equally high, move on to Chapter 3.

If you answered 4–7 questions correctly, you know how to use context to determine meaning, but you need more practice to really sharpen this skill. Work through the quiz at the end of the chapter to check your progress.

If you answered 1–3 questions correctly, you have difficulty using context to determine the meaning of unfamiliar words. Study the lesson that follows carefully, and do the practice quiz on a separate sheet of paper so that you can do the exercise several times if necessary. Consider supplementing your test preparation with some reading comprehension practice. Try LearningExpress's *501 Reading Comprehension Questions, 2nd edition.*

JUST IN TIME LESSON— DETERMINING MEANING FROM CONTEXT

SHORTCUT: BE AN ACTIVE READER

Active reading is one of the most important vocabulary and reading comprehension skill-building strategies you can employ, and it is a skill you can practice every day. As you read the daily newspaper, your favorite magazine, or a good book, have a dictionary handy. Look up as many unfamiliar words as you can so that your bank of vocabulary words becomes as large as it can be.

This may sound like a contradiction, but if you make a habit of taking the time to read carefully and actively, you will actually spend *less* time learning the meaning of new vocabulary words. By reading carefully, you will often be able to determine meaning from context. By reading actively, you will continually expand your bank of vocabulary words—and the bigger your word base, the more you will comprehend, and the less time you will spend looking up words.

Ever since you were learning your first words, you have been determining meaning from context. **Context** refers to the words and sentences that surround a particular word and help fix its meaning. For example, notice how the context of the sentence below helps give the word *candor* its meaning:

I admire Arun's *candor*, but sometimes he can be a bit *too* honest.

Candor means:
a. attitude.
b. frank, sincere speech.
c. readiness to judge or criticize others.
d. comfort speaking in front of people.
e. irritability.

GLOSSARY

CONTEXT the words and sentences that surround a word or phrase and help convey its meaning

Based on the context of the sentence, only **b** can be the correct answer. The speaker tells you that Arun is sometimes *too* honest, thus signifying that *candor* means frank, sincere speech—Arun tells people exactly what he thinks.

 RULE BOOK: USE IT OR LOSE IT

There's really only one "rule" for building your vocabulary: *Use it or lose it.* When you are learning a new word, if you don't use it, you will soon forget what it means. Write new words down on a vocabulary list. Use them in emails or letters to friends. Introduce them to members of your family. Use the words you learn in your everyday communications as much as possible so they become a permanent part of your vocabulary.

Even if you can't figure out exactly what *candor* means, you can tell from the context whether it is something positive or negative, and this can help you narrow down your answer choices on an exam. In this case, because the speaker admires Arun's candor, you can assume that candor is a positive thing. You can therefore eliminate choices **c** and **e**.

There are four types of context clues that can help you:

1. Restatement
2. Positive/Negative
3. Contrast
4. Specific Detail

This sentence, then, uses two types of context clues: **restatement** and **positive/negative**. The first part of the sentence tells you that candor is a good thing (positive/negative) while the second part essentially restates the meaning of the word. Here's another example of a sentence that uses these two types of context clues:

> Hani suddenly found himself *destitute*, so poor that he could barely afford to eat.

The context clearly reveals that *destitute* is not a positive word; it is not a good thing to be so poor one can barely afford to eat. The context also restates the meaning of *destitute*, essentially defining the word within the sentence, so that you can tell exactly what *destitute* means: extremely poor.

There are two other types of context clues to watch for. Read the following paragraph as an example (but *don't* look up the italicized words!):

> Sarah had worked so hard for the past few weeks that she decided she owed herself a day of complete *indolence*. Saturday, she slept until noon, ordered take-out so she wouldn't have to cook, and left the dishes in the sink. She left her chores for another day and spent the afternoon lying on the couch, reading and watching television. But on Sunday, she was back to her old *assiduous* self, and by noon she had already cleaned her whole apartment, done her grocery shopping, and paid her bills.

How do you know what *indolence* means? From two more types of context clues: **contrast** and **specific detail**. The first sentence suggests that *indolence* is in contrast to working hard, while the second and third sentences confirm this with specific details. Thus you can determine that *indolence* means:

a. luxury.
b. hard labor.
c. deep sleep.
d. laziness.
e. household chores.

The answer is **d**, laziness. The specific details tell you that Sarah did her best to laze around the house all day. Besides, you know the other answers are incorrect because Sarah didn't do anything luxurious (choice **a**) and she didn't do any work or chores (choices **b** and **e**). There's no mention of sleep in the paragraph, so choice **c** is also incorrect.

Now let's look at the context in which *assiduous* is used. Again, you have two kinds of context clues: contrast and specific detail. You know that the *assiduous* Sarah of Sunday was very different from the *indolent* Sarah of Saturday (contrast). You also know what the *assiduous* Sarah does: she is very, very busy on Sunday, cleaning and working around the house (specific detail). *Assiduous* means diligent, hardworking; persevering, unremitting.

▶ *Denotation and Connotation*

You already know that some words have more than one meaning. A *quack*, for example, is the sound a duck makes, but a quack is also an untrained or unqualified person who pretends to be a doctor. But words also have another meaning beyond their **denotation** or dictionary definition. Each word also has a **connotation**—an implied meaning or emotional impact.

For example, if you were to look up the word *playful* in the dictionary, you might get a definition similar to that of two of its synonyms, *spirited* and *mischievous*. But all three of these words have different connotations and bring to mind different feelings. *Spirited* has a positive connotation and *mischievous* a negative connotation while *playful* is neutral in tone.

GLOSSARY

DENOTATION a word's exact meaning or dictionary definition
CONNOTATION a word's implied meaning or emotional impact

When you come across an unfamiliar word, the context will often reveal a great deal about the connotation of that word, even if it does not provide enough information for you to determine its denotation. At a minimum, the connotations of the surrounding words will usually tell you whether the vocabulary word is positive or negative. Therefore, when you are looking for context clues, make sure you look at the surrounding words carefully and consider their denotations and connotations.

▶ *How Much Context Do You Need?*

In the passage about Sarah, you would still be able to understand the main idea of the passage even if you did not know—or could not figure out—the meanings of *indolence* and *assiduous*. In some cases, though, your understanding of a sentence or paragraph depends on your understanding of a particular word or phrase. For example, you can't understand what *inept* means from the sentence below—it simply does not provide sufficient context. In fact, you can't even figure out if it is something positive or negative, because the sentence provides almost no context at all:

Sabina is an utterly *inept* dancer.

Is Sabina a *graceful* dancer? An *awkward* dancer? Or an *accomplished* dancer? You simply cannot tell from the context. But you *could* figure out what *inept* means by breaking down the word into its prefix (*in*) and word root (*ept*). That's the subject of the next three lessons. Meanwhile, however, here's a sentence that does give you the context you need to determine the meaning of the word:

Despite years of lessons, Sabina remains an utterly *inept* dancer who simply stumbles across the dance floor.

Now we can tell through context that *inept* means *awkward* or *clumsy*. Being able to determine the meaning of unfamiliar words from their context is an essential vocabulary skill. Sometimes you will find unfamiliar words whose meanings are indecipherable without a dictionary. More often than not, though, a careful look at the context will give you enough clues to interpret the definitions.

EXTRA HELP

If your Benchmark Quiz score was low (less than four correct answers) or you feel the need for more practice determining meaning from context, you can find extra help in these other LearningExpress titles:

Vocabulary and Spelling Success in 20 Minutes a Day, 3rd edition. Each of the 20 vocabulary lessons provides vocabulary in context exercises.

Reading Comprehension Success in 20 Minutes a Day, 2nd edition. Lesson 3 provides a lesson on determining vocabulary in context.

501 Vocabulary Questions offers more practice, too.

TIPS AND STRATEGIES

Vocabulary-in-context questions are common on standardized tests. Here are some specific tips and strategies to use while preparing for and taking the exam:

- Remember that determining meaning from context is a vocabulary skill you have been using all of your life. This is something you *know* how to do.
- On any vocabulary-in-context question on an exam, there *will* be some kind of context clue to help you determine meaning. Remember the four types: **restatement, positive/negative, contrast**, and **specific detail.**
- Remember that you have a very powerful tool on a multiple-choice exam: the process of elimination. From the start, you can usually eliminate one or two answers that you know are incorrect. For example, you can eliminate negative choices if the context suggests the word is positive.
- To help you eliminate answers, read the sentence with each answer choice substituted for the vocabulary word. Often, putting the word in the context of the sentence can help you determine whether an answer is right or wrong.
- Be sure to look carefully at the context of the sentence itself and avoid bringing your own contextual meaning from your own experiences of colloquial language use, or slang.

- Consider the tone and connotation of the other words in the sentence. At minimum, this can often help you determine whether the vocabulary word is positive or negative.
- Look for introductory words and phrases such as *unfortunately, however, surprisingly*. These words often tell you whether the word is positive or negative and/or set up contrast clues.
- Read carefully. Look for specific details that provide clues to meaning.
- If you have heard the vocabulary word before but aren't sure what it means, try to remember the context in which you heard it used before. This may help you better use the context as it is presented on the exam.

PRACTICE

For each question below, use the context of the sentence to determine the meaning of the italicized word.

1. The editor, preferring a more *terse* writing style, cut 500 words from the 2,000-word article.

   Terse means:
   a. elegant.
   b. factual.
   c. descriptive.
   d. concise.
   e. innovative.

2. Victor Frankenstein spent the last years of his life chasing his *elusive* monster, who was always one step of his creator.

   Elusive means:
   a. unable to be compared.
   b. unable to be captured.
   c. unable to be forgotten.
   d. unable to be avoided.
   e. unable to be accepted.

3. Xiu's timely joke served to *diffuse* the tension in the room, and the rest of the meeting was highly productive.

Diffuse means:
a. refuse.
b. intensify.
c. create.
d. soften.
e. thicken.

4. I completely lost track of Tula's point because she kept *digressing* to unrelated topics.

Digress means:
a. to deviate, stray.
b. to regress, revert.
c. to change the tone.
d. to express concisely.
e. to repeat, reiterate.

5. The senator *evaded* the question by changing the subject and accusing his opponent of misconduct.

Evade means:
a. to escape or elude.
b. to answer indirectly.
c. to refuse to answer directly.
d. to deceive.
e. to challenge.

6. Samantha hasn't said why she's been so withdrawn lately, but I would *surmise* that it is because she is still upset about not being able to go to camp.

Surmise means:
a. confirm.
b. surprise.
c. believe.
d. deny.
e. guess.

7. The details can be worked out later; what's important is that we agree with the *crux* of my argument, which is that everyone should be held equally accountable.

Crux means:
a. overall tone.
b. specific fact.
c. main point.
d. logic, reasoning.
e. persuasiveness.

8. Marty kept interrupting the meeting with remarks that were not only *tangential* but downright irrelevant.

Tangential means:
a. loosely related.
b. rude and obnoxious.
c. very important.
d. thoughtful, intelligent.
e. obtuse, not intelligent.

9. Sunil *honed* his public speaking skills by practicing in front of a mirror each day until he felt confident about his abilities.

Hone means:
a. to make a habit of.
b. to sharpen or improve.
c. to reveal, make public.
d. to express clearly.
e. to do repeatedly.

10. The evidence was *incontrovertible*, and the jury found the defendant guilty on all charges.

Incontrovertible means:
a. questionable.
b. illegally obtained.
c. indisputable.
d. circumstantial.
e. inconclusive.

11. After listening to the couple speak for a few minutes, Eleanor quickly *discerned* that the underlying problem in their relationship was a lack of trust.

Discern means:
a. to state clearly.
b. to deceive.
c. to complicate.
d. to perceive.
e. to believe.

12. Ivan was writing an article for people who know nothing about computers, so he had to be sure he didn't use any *jargon* that would confuse readers.

Jargon means:
a. insulting or derogatory language.
b. technical or specialized terminology.
c. slangy, informal speech.
d. sophisticated vocabulary.
e. computer-related jokes.

13. Adolfo often dresses in a rather *eccentric* way, but his beliefs are as conservative as can be.

Eccentric means:
a. standard, status quo.
b. peculiar, uncommon.
c. outmoded, out of style.
d. bright and cheerful.
e. of the highest quality, top-notch.

14. To Hannah, who had never been on a ranch, Ted's job seemed glamorous and exotic, but Ted, who had lived on a ranch his whole life, thought the work was rather *mundane*.

Mundane means:
a. exceptional.
b. exhausting.
c. dirty.
d. underpaid.
e. ordinary.

15. Matthew launched into a *tirade* when he discovered that his roommate had once again borrowed something without asking—and broken it.

Tirade means:
a. an escape.
b. a quiet discussion.
c. a nostalgic reverie.
d. a long, angry speech.
e. an amusing anecdote.

16. Although there are dozens of books about Jesse James, *Outlaw* stands out among the others for its *novel* approach to the subject.

Novel means:
a. timely.
b. original.
c. literary.
d. standard.
e. radical.

17. Jorge's constant flattery *deluded* Sheila into believing that she was perfect.

Delude means:
a. to remind.
b. to force.
c. to pressure.
d. to release.
e. to deceive.

18. Although Trevor is unsure of his talent, he has a real *penchant* for drawing, so he plans to apply to art school.

Penchant means:
a. strong liking.
b. habit or routine.
c. opportunity.
d. distaste.
e. education.

19. Remembering with fear the German shepherd who bit him long ago, Aidan gave the poodle a *wary* glance.

Wary means:
a. tender, loving.
b. evil, hateful.
c. angry, vengeful.
d. guarded, cautious.
e. indifferent.

20. My attempt to make a special anniversary dinner was a complete *debacle*, and we ended up just ordering Chinese food.

Debacle means:
a. great success.
b. gourmet cooking.
c. total disaster.
d. amateur behavior.
e. a lesson well learned.

21. Although he meant it as a compliment, Jordan's remark that Imani's poem was "unusual" *incensed* her, and she stormed out of the room.

Incense means:
a. to please.
b. to anger.
c. to reinforce.
d. to burn.
e. to criticize.

22. Caleigh hated the fact that I was her superior, and she was constantly trying to *undermine* my authority by openly challenging every decision I made.

Undermine means:
a. to weaken.
b. to reinforce.
c. to take over.
d. to scatter.
e. to elevate.

23. Because Candace neglected to study and stayed out late the night before her exam, she was expecting an *abysmal* score.

Abysmal means:
a. outstanding.
b. positive.
c. slightly lower than usual.
d. extremely bad.
e. uncharacteristic.

24. Because of the large number of proposals we received, we will only be able to give each one a *cursory* review.

Cursory means:
a. thorough, detailed.
b. primary.
c. hasty and careless.
d. performed on a computer.
e. done out of a sense of duty.

25. Fernanda was in a *pensive* mood as she tried to determine the best way to resolve her difficulties.

Pensive means:
a. joyous.
b. deeply thoughtful.
c. indifferent.
d. irrational.
e. light-hearted.

ANSWERS

1. d. *Terse* means concise, using no unnecessary words. The main clue is that the editor cut the article by 25%, dramatically reducing its wordiness.

2. b. *Elusive* means evasive, eluding the grasp; difficult to capture. The sentence tells you that Dr. Frankenstein was never able to catch the creature, who constantly escaped his grasp.

3. d. To *diffuse* means to spread throughout, disperse; to soften or make less brilliant. Xiu's joke softened the tension so that the meeting could be more productive.

4. a. To *digress* means to turn aside, deviate; to stray from the main subject in writing or speaking. The speaker loses track of the point because Tula keeps shifting from the main topic to unrelated subjects.

5. a. To *evade* means to elude or avoid by cleverness or deceit; to avoid fulfilling, answering, or doing. The senator avoids answering the question by changing the subject.

6. e. To *surmise* means to infer based upon insufficient evidence, to guess. The speaker is guessing why Samantha is upset; he doesn't know for sure, though, because Samantha hasn't explained her withdrawal.

7. c. *Crux* means the central or critical point or feature, especially of a problem. The main context clue is that the speaker isn't concerned with the details but is focused on getting agreement on the main point.

8. a. *Tangential* means only superficially relevant; of no substantive connection. Marty's comments are not only tangential but "downright irrelevant," which means that they are at best loosely related to the topic.

9. b. *Hone* means to sharpen; to perfect, make more effective. The sentence tells you that Sunil practiced daily, indicating that he wanted to improve his public speaking skills.

10. c. *Incontrovertible* means indisputable, undeniable. Because the jury found the defendant guilty, you can infer that the evidence was indisputable.

11. d. *Discern* means to perceive clearly, to distinguish as being distinct. Eleanor is able to determine the problem through observing the couple.

12. b. *Jargon* is the specialized or technical language of a specific trade or group. Because Ivan's readers are people who know nothing about computers, he cannot use terminology used by the computer-savvy; thus, he must avoid jargon.

13. b. *Eccentric* means deviating from the conventional or established norm; anomalous, irregular. The context sets up a contrast between *eccentric* and conventional.

14. e. *Mundane* means ordinary, commonplace, dull. The context sets up a contrast between Hannah's impression of Ted's job (glamorous and exotic) and Ted's impression of his own job (ordinary, dull).

15. d. A *tirade* is a long, angry, highly critical speech. The context suggests that Matthew is angry with his roommate, who has repeatedly taken things without asking, and this time has even broken something. He is therefore likely to speak in an angry, critical way.

16. b. *Novel* means strikingly new, original, or different. The context sets up a contrast between the dozens of other books and *Outlaw*, which approaches the topic in a new way.

17. e. *Delude* means to deceive, make someone believe something that is wrong. Of course, no one is perfect, so the context makes it clear that Sheila is being deceived into believing something that is not true. In addition, there is no indication of force or pressure on Sheila; flattery is a softer, more subtle kind of persuasion.

18. a. A *penchant* is a strong liking or inclination for something. Trevor is unsure of his ability, but he plans to apply to art school anyway—this suggests that he enjoys drawing a great deal.

19. d. *Wary* means guarded, watchful, cautious. Aidan's past experience would logically make him cautious around dogs.

20. c. A *debacle* is a total defeat or failure, a sudden disaster or collapse. The fact that the speaker ended up ordering Chinese food for dinner—when an elaborate home-cooked meal had been planned—indicates that the speaker's meal was unsuccessful. The other key context clue is the word *attempt*, which indicates that the dinner was a failure.

21. b. To *incense* is to make someone angry. The context sets up a contrast between Jordan's attempt to compliment Imani and her reaction (storming out of the room), which indicates that she was angry or upset.

22. a. To *undermine* is to weaken or injure; to destroy in an underhanded way. The context tells you what motivates Caleigh's behavior—she hates the fact that the speaker is her superior—so she attempts to weaken his authority by openly challenging his decisions.

23. d. *Abysmal* means extreme, limitless, profound; extremely bad. The context tells you that Candace did not study and did not sleep well the night before the exam; these two facts combined explain why she would expect a very bad score.

24. c. *Cursory* means hasty and superficial. The context suggests as conflict between the number of proposals and the amount of time in which they can be reviewed.

25. b. *Pensive* means deeply thoughtful, especially in a serious or melancholy manner. If Fernanda is trying to work out a problem, she is likely to be seriously thoughtful. The context does not allow for joyous, indifferent, or lighthearted response, and it suggests that she is rationally trying to think things through (determining the best response).

WORD LIST

abysmal (ă·'biz·măl) *adj.* 1. extreme, limitless, profound 2. extremely bad. *Related word:* **abyss**.

assiduous (ă·'sij·oo·ŭs) *adj.* diligent, hardworking; persevering, unremitting.

benign (bi·'nīn) *adj.* 1. gentle, mild, kind; having a beneficial or favorable nature or influence 2. not harmful or malignant.

candor ('kan·dŏr) *n.* frank, sincere speech; openness. *Related word:* **candid**.

caustic ('kaws·tik) *adj.* 1. able to burn, corrode, or dissolve by chemical action 2. bitingly sarcastic, cutting.

crux (kruks) *n.* the central or critical point or feature, especially of a problem.

cursory ('kur·sŏ·ree) *adj.* hasty and superficial.

debacle (di·'bah·kěl) *n.* 1. a sudden disaster or collapse; a total defeat or failure 2. a sudden breaking up or breaking loose; violent flood waters, often caused by the breaking up of ice in a river.

delude (di·'lood) *v.* to deceive, make someone believe something that is wrong. *Related word:* **delusion**.

destitute ('des·ti·toot) *adj.* 1. penniless, extremely poor 2. utterly lacking.

diffuse (di·'fyooz) *v.* 1. to spread throughout, disperse, extend 2. to soften, make less brilliant; (di·'fyoos) *adj.* 1. spread out, scattered, not concentrated 2. wordy, verbose.

digress (di·'gres) *v.* to turn aside, deviate, or swerve; to stray from the main subject in writing or speaking.

discern (di·'surn) *v.* to perceive clearly; to distinguish, recognize as being distinct.

eccentric (ik·'sen·trik) *adj.* deviating from the conventional or established norm or pattern; anomalous, irregular.

elusive (i·'loo·siv) *adj.* evasive, eluding the grasp; difficult to capture, describe or comprehend.

emulate ('em·yŭ·layt) *v.* to try to equal or excel, especially by imitation.

enigma (ĕ·'nig·mă) *n.* something that is puzzling or difficult to understand; a baffling problem or riddle.

evade (i·'vayd) *v.* to elude or avoid by cleverness or deceit 2. to avoid fulfilling, answering, or doing. *Related word:* **evasion**.

explicit (ik·'splis·it) *adj.* stated clearly and fully; straightforward, exact.

futile ('fyoo·tǐl) *adj.* useless, producing no result; hopeless, vain.

garner ('gahr·něr) *v.* to gather and store up; to amass, acquire.

hone (hohn) *v.* to sharpen; to perfect, make more effective.

incense (in·'sens) *v.* to make (someone) angry.

incontrovertible (in·kon·trŏ·'vur·tĭ·bĕl) *adj.* indisputable, undeniable.

indolent ('in·dŏ·lĕnt) *adj.* 1. lazy, lethargic, inclined to avoid labor 2. causing little or no pain; slow to grow or heal.

inept (in·'ept) *adj.* 1. not suitable, inappropriate 2. absurd, foolish 3. incompetent, bungling and clumsy.

jargon ('jahr·gŏn) *n.* 1. specialized or technical language of a specific trade or group 2. nonsensical or meaningless talk.

mundane (mun·'dayn) *adj.* ordinary, commonplace, dull 2. worldly, secular, not spiritual.

novel ('nov·ĕl) *adj.* strikingly new, original, or different. *Related word:* ***novelty***.

penchant ('pen·chănt) *n.* a strong liking or inclination (for something).

pensive ('pen·siv) *adj.* deeply thoughtful, especially in a serious or melancholy manner.

surmise (sŭr·'mīz) *v.* to infer based upon insufficient evidence; to guess, conjecture.

tangential (tan·'jen·shăl) *adj.* 1. only superficially relevant; of no substantive connection 2. of or relating to a tanget.

teem (teem) *v.* to be full of; to be present in large numbers.

terse (turs) *adj.* concise, using no unnecessary words, succinct.

thwart (thwort) *v.* to prevent the accomplishment or realization of something.

tirade ('tī·rayd) *n.* a long, angry, often highly critical speech; a violent denunciation or condemnation.

trite (trīt) *adj.* repeated too often, overly familiar through overuse; worn out, hackneyed.

undermine (un·dĕr·'mīn) *v.* 1. to weaken or injure, especially by wearing away at the foundation 2. to destroy in an underhanded way.

wary (wair·ee) *adj.* guarded, watchful, cautious.

Using Prefixes and Suffixes

When you come across unfamiliar words without context, breaking those words into their parts can help you determine their meaning. This lesson reviews prefixes and suffixes and how you can use them to add new words to your vocabulary—and better understand words you already know. Before you begin learning and reviewing prefixes and suffixes, take a few minutes to take this ten-question *Benchmark Quiz*. These questions are similar to the type of questions that you will find on important tests. When you are finished, check the answer key carefully to assess your results. Your Benchmark Quiz analysis will help you determine how much time you need to spend on prefixes and suffixes as well as the specific words you need to learn in order to increase your vocabulary power. A complete list of the vocabulary words used in this lesson is provided at the end of this chapter.

BENCHMARK QUIZ

Choose the best answer to each question using your knowledge of prefixes and suffixes.

1. *Antecedent* means:
   a. fighting against.
   b. looking after.
   c. coming before.
   d. under the authority of.
   e. recent.

2. *Multifaceted* means:
   a. two-faced.
   b. many sided.
   c. uniform.
   d. cut into parts.
   e. chaotic.

3. *Circumspect* means:
   a. relating to the circus.
   b. to examine thoroughly.
   c. put forth in writing.
   d. in an uncomfortable position.
   e. looking around carefully.

4. *Consensus* means:
   a. general agreement by a group.
   b. an individual opinion.
   c. a counting of individuals.
   d. to issue a warning.
   e. separate and dissimilar.

5. *Supercilious* means:
   a. less than the norm, disappointing.
   b. exactly as expected.
   c. speaking in a measured, exact tone.
   d. haughty, with an air of superiority.
   e. achieving what one intended to achieve.

6. To *presage* means:
   a. to warn in advance.
   b. to send a message.
   c. to pressure.
   d. to age gracefully.
   e. to be slow to realize.

7. *Dubious* means:
   a. one who doubts, a non-believer.
   b. to doubt or question.
   c. doubtful, questionable.
   d. to be uncertain.
   e. uncertainty, doubt.

8. *Agrarian* means:
   a. incapable of making a decision.
   b. to cultivate.
   c. to be out of date.
   d. relating to land or land ownership.
   e. the process of testing for impurities.

9. *Parity* means:
   a. to make equal in status, amount, or degree.
   b. the state of being equal in status, amount, or degree.
   c. one who is equal in status, amount, or degree.
   d. the act of making someone or something equal in status, amount, or degree.
   e. to cause to become equal in status, amount, or degree.

10. *Galvanize* means:
    a. to be active or aware.
    b. the state of becoming active or aware.
    c. one who becomes active or aware.
    d. the act of making someone or something become active or aware.
    e. to cause to become active or aware.

BENCHMARK QUIZ SOLUTIONS

How did you do on remembering prefixes and suffixes? Check your answers here, and then analyze the results to figure out your plan of attack for mastering these topics.

▶ *Answers*

1. **c.** The prefix *ante-* means before. *Antecedent* means that which precedes; the thing, circumstance, or event that came before.

2. b. The prefix *multi-* means many. *Multifaceted* means having many facets or aspects; complex.

3. e. The prefix *circum-* means around, on all sides. *Circumspect* means cautious, wary, watchful.

4. a. The prefix *con-* means with, together. *Consensus* means general agreement or accord; an opinion or position reached by a group.

5. d. The prefix *super-* means above, over, or exceeding. *Supercilious* means with an air of superiority (as if one is above or better than another); haughty, scornful, disdainful.

6. a. The prefix *pre-* means before. To *presage* means to indicate or warn of in advance; to predict, foretell.

7. c. The adjective suffix *-ous* means having the quality of, relating to. *Dubious* means doubtful, questionable; fraught with uncertainty, wavering.

8. d. The adjective suffix *-ian* means one who is or does, related to. *Agrarian* means relating to or concerning land and its ownership or cultivation.

9. b. The noun suffix *-ity* means state of being. *Parity* means having equality in status, amount, value or degree; equivalence.

10. e. The verb suffix *-ize* means to cause, to bring about. To *galvanize* means to stimulate or rouse into awareness or action.

BENCHMARK QUIZ RESULTS

If you answered 8–10 questions correctly, well done! You are already skilled at using prefixes and suffixes to determine meaning. Give the lesson a quick review and do the practice exercise. If your score on the practice test is equally high, move on to Chapter 4.

If you answered 4–7 questions correctly, you are familiar with some of the most common prefixes and suffixes and how to use them to determine meaning. But you need more practice to really sharpen this skill. Be sure to set aside some time to carefully review the complete list of common prefixes and suffixes located in Appendix A.

If you answered 1–3 questions correctly, perhaps it has been a while since you reviewed prefixes and suffixes, or perhaps English is not your primary language. Study the lesson that follows carefully, and do the practice quiz on a separate sheet of paper so that you can do the exercise several times if necessary. Take extra time to learn the complete list of common prefixes and suffixes located in Appendix A.

JUST IN TIME LESSON—PREFIXES AND SUFFIXES

A good knowledge of prefixes and suffixes is essential to building an effective vocabulary. The more familiar you are with these fundamental word parts, the easier it will be to determine the meaning of unfamiliar words.

There are dozens of prefixes and suffixes in the English language. The good news is that you probably already know a majority of them and use them every day without even thinking about it. This lesson will review some of the most common prefixes and suffixes so that you can use them to understand the meaning of new vocabulary words.

IF ENGLISH IS NOT YOUR PRIMARY LANGUAGE

Learning prefixes and suffixes in another language may seem like a daunting task, but the job may be easier than you think. Though prefixes and suffixes often appear in books like this with sophisticated vocabulary words, you are already using the same prefixes and suffixes with simple words that you already know well. In the prefix and suffix lists, both in this chapter and in the appendix, everyday examples have been provided for you, rather than the kind of vocabulary words you are likely to see on an exam. This will help you more easily memorize the prefix and suffix meanings.

PREFIXES

Prefixes are syllables attached to the beginning of words to change or add to the meaning of the root word in some way. For example, the word *prefix* itself uses the prefix *pre-*, meaning before. Thus the meaning of the root word, *fix*, changes:

> *fix:* to place securely or firmly
> *prefix:* something placed at the beginning of a word

Several of the vocabulary words you studied in Chapter 2 used prefixes, including *incontrovertible* and *inept*, which both use the prefix *in-*, meaning *not*—not disputable and not suitable or competent.

Knowledge of prefixes can help you in many ways as you build your vocabulary and as you take your exam. Although you can't determine meaning based on a prefix alone—you also need to know the root of the word—you *can* often use a prefix to determine whether a word is positive or negative, to eliminate incorrect answers, and to provide partial context for the meaning of the word. For example, take the word *polyglot*. If you know that the prefix *poly-* means many, you can eliminate all but the correct answer in the question below:

A *polyglot* is:
a. someone who is an expert in global issues.
b. someone who administers lie detector tests.
c. someone who is easily frightened.
d. someone who speaks many languages.
e. someone who travels.

Choice **d** is the only answer that includes the idea of *many* or *multiple*. Thus, it is the only possible correct answer.

GLOSSARY

ROOT the main part of a word; the base upon which prefixes and suffixes are added
PREFIX syllable(s) attached to the beginning of a word to change or add to its meaning
SUFFIX syllable(s) attached to the end of a word to change or add to its meaning

You will not always be so lucky as to eliminate all of the incorrect answers, but even eliminating two or three will be a great help. For example, knowing that the prefix *mal-* means bad, evil, or wrong can help you significantly narrow down your choices in the following question:

To *malign* means:
a. to arrange.
b. to speak badly about.
c. to charm, enchant.
d. to cast an evil spell.
e. to flatter.

With your knowledge of prefixes, you can eliminate choices **a**, **c**, and **e**, leaving you with a 50-50 chance of choosing the correct answer. If you recall any context in which you have heard the word *malign* before, you may be able to choose the correct answer, **b**. To *malign* is to say evil, harmful, and often untrue things about someone; to speak ill of.

Below you will find a list of the prefixes for the vocabulary words in this lesson. For each prefix, we have provided two examples of words that use that prefix. With a few exceptions, these examples are not test-prep words;

rather, they are basic words that are probably already part of your vocabulary. This will help you remember the meaning of each prefix—and show you just how well you already know them.

a, an: not, without
amoral (not moral), *atypical* (not typical)

ab, abs: from, away, off
abduct (to take by force), *abnormal* (away from or apart from the standard)

ante: prior to, in front of, before
anterior (placed before), *antedate* (to proceed in time, come before)

anti, ant: opposite, opposing, against
antibiotic (substance that kills microorganisms), *antidote* (remedy for counteracting the effects of a poison),

circ, circum: around, about, on all sides
circumference (the outer boundary of a circle), *circumstance* (the conditions or state of affairs surrounding or affecting an event; a particular incident or occurrence)

co, com, con: with, together, jointly
cooperate (to work together, comply), *connect* (to bind or fasten together)

dis: away from, apart, reversal, not
dismiss (to send away from, eject), *disobedient* (not obedient)

ex: out, out of, away from
exit (go out), *expel* (to drive out or away)

in: not
inaccurate (not accurate), *informal* (not formal)

inter: between, among, within
intercept (to stop someone or something between its starting point and destination), *intervene* (to come, occur, appear, or lie between two points of time or things)

mal: bad, abnormal, evil, wrong
malfunction (to fail to function properly), *malpractice* (wrongdoing, especially improper or negligent treatment of a patient by a physician)

mis: bad, wrong, ill; opposite or lack of
misbehave (to behave badly), *misspell* (to spell incorrectly)

multi: many, multiple
multimedia (the combined use of several media), *multiple* (having several or many parts or elements)

neo: new, recent, a new form of
neonatal (of or relating to a newborn child), *neologism* (a new word or phrase)

non: not
nonfiction (the genre of literature that includes all types of books other than fiction), *nonsmoker* (someone who does not smoke)

poly: many, much

polygamy (the system of having more than one wife at a time), *polysyllabic* (having three or more syllables)

pre: before

precaution (something done in advance to avoid risk), *predict* (to forecast, make known in advance)

re: back, again

rebuild (to build again after destruction), *replace* (to put back in its former position; to take the place of)

sub: under, beneath, below

subdue (to overcome, bring under control), *submarine* (a ship that can operate under water)

super: above, over, exceeding

superb (grand, magnificent, of unusually high quality, excellent), *superman* (a man with powers exceeding ordinary human capacity)

uni: one

unify (to form into a single unit, unite), *unite* (to join together, make or become one)

A more comprehensive list of the most common English prefixes is located in Appendix A. After you have completed this lesson, make sure you review the list carefully and study any prefixes that are unfamiliar to you.

SOUNDS LIKE . . .

As you use your knowledge of prefixes and suffixes to determine meaning, see if you can recall hearing or using any words with similar roots or sounds. For example, when you were taking the Benchmark Quiz, you may have realized that *agrarian* sounds like it shares a root word with *agriculture*—and it does. Even if you don't know exactly what *agriculture* means, you might know that it has something to do with land and its cultivation. Thus you would have been able to more quickly narrow down the answer choices to **b** (to cultivate) and **d** (relating to land or land ownership). Once you realize that the suffix *-ian* calls for an adjective, not a verb, then you can eliminate **b** and choose the correct answer, **d**.

SUFFIXES

Suffixes are syllables added to the end of words to change or add to their meaning. They often change a word's part of speech, thereby also changing how the word functions in a sentence. Suffixes tell you whether a word is a person, place, or thing (a **noun**); an action or state of being (a **verb**); or a modifier, which is a word that describes (an **adjective** or **adverb**).

PARTS OF SPEECH—A QUICK REVIEW

The following table offers a quick reference guide for the main parts of speech.

PART OF SPEECH	FUNCTION	EXAMPLES
noun	names a person, place, thing, or concept	*cloud, Helen, car, Elm Court, brush, valor*
verb	shows an action, occurrence, or state of being	*go, jump, feel, imagine, interrupt*
adjective	describes nouns and pronouns; can also identify or quantify; tells what kind, which one, how many, how much	*white, oblong, ancient, exhilarating that (e.g., that dog) several (e.g., several dogs)*
adverb	describes verbs, adjectives, other adverbs, or entire clauses; tells where, when, how and to what extent	*slowly, clumsily, never, very, here, soon*

For example, look how the suffixes below change the word *antagonist* from a noun to an adjective to a verb (and don't forget to notice the prefix, *ant-*):

antagonist	noun	one who opposes or contends with another; an adversary, opponent
antagonistic	adjective	opposing, combating, adversarial
antagonize	verb	to oppose actively, contend; to provoke the hostility of

Likewise, the word *venerate* changes from a verb to an adjective to a noun, depending upon its suffix:

venerate	verb	to regard with deep respect or reverence; to honor with a sense of awe, revere
venerable	adjective	worthy of deep respect or reverence; deserving of honor and respect
venerator	noun	one who shows deep respect or reverence

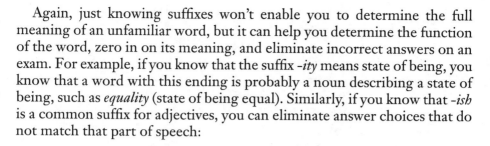

Again, just knowing suffixes won't enable you to determine the full meaning of an unfamiliar word, but it can help you determine the function of the word, zero in on its meaning, and eliminate incorrect answers on an exam. For example, if you know that the suffix *-ity* means state of being, you know that a word with this ending is probably a noun describing a state of being, such as *equality* (state of being equal). Similarly, if you know that *-ish* is a common suffix for adjectives, you can eliminate answer choices that do not match that part of speech:

Squeamish means:
a. to scream or squeal.
b. recurring illness.
c. extremely shy.
d. easily disgusted.
e. the belief that animals have rights similar to humans.

Choices **a**, **b**, and **e** are definitions for other parts of speech—a verb, a noun, and another noun, respectively. Only choices **c** and **d** define adjectives, and only choice **d** is correct. *Squeamish* means easily sickened, disgusted, nauseated or shocked.

 RULE BOOK: MOST OF THE TIME, BUT NOT ALWAYS

While prefixes and suffixes are fundamental components of our vocabulary, it's important to remember that they are tools to use in conjunction with other vocabulary skills. For example, *vanquish* and *varnish* both end in *-ish*, but they are both verbs, not adjectives.

But most words that end in *-ish* are adjectives describing a characteristic. Thus, as you come across vocabulary words with common prefixes and suffixes, use your knowledge of prefixes and suffixes, but look for other clues to meaning as well, including context (see Chapter 2) and word roots (see Chapters 3, 4, and Appendix A) to be sure you are on the right track.

Here is a list of the suffixes you need to know for the practice exercises in this lesson. For each suffix, we have again provided two examples of words that use that suffix, and again, these examples are basic words that are part of your everyday vocabulary.

▶ *Noun Suffixes*

-ance, -ence: action, process, or state of
   adolescence (the state of growing up from childhood to adulthood;

the transitional period between youth and maturity), *dependence* (the state of being dependent)

-ion: act or process; state or condition
detection (the act of detecting), *election* (the act or power of electing)

-ism: act, practice, or process; state or doctrine of
feminism (belief in the social, political, and economic equality of the sexes), *materialism* (the belief that the acquisition of material possessions is the highest good)

-ist: one who (performs, makes, produces, believes, etc.)
dentist (one who is trained and licensed to practice dentistry), *pianist* (one who plays the piano)

-ity: quality, state, or degree
equality (the state or quality of being equal), *fidelity* (the quality of being faithful)

-sis: process or action
diagnosis (the process of identifying the nature or cause of a disease or injury), *paralysis* (loss of sensation or ability to move or function)

-ure: act, condition, process, function
enclosure (the act of enclosing or state of being enclosed), *failure* (the condition or act of not achieving a desired end; the act or fact of failing to perform as expected or requested)

SHORT CUT

You may try to kill two birds with one stone by memorizing a difficult vocabulary word for each prefix or suffix. However, you can quickly and accurately learn the most common prefixes and suffixes by remembering examples of words you already know, such as *cooperate* and *dismiss*. Because the words are already so familiar to you, you don't have to worry about forgetting their meaning and you will be able to recall them easily even while under the pressure of an exam.

▶ *Adjective Suffixes*

-able, -ible: capable or worthy of; tending or liable to
dependable (worthy of being depended on, trustworthy), *incredible* (not credible; unable to be believed, improbable)

-al, -ial, ical: having the quality of, relating to, or characterized by
practical (of or relating to practice or action; useful), *ethical* (of or relating to ethics or morals)

-an, -ian: one who is or does; related to, characteristic of
humanitarian (one who is devoted to the promotion of human welfare; relating to, or characteristic of a humanitarian), *politician* (one who seeks or holds a political office)

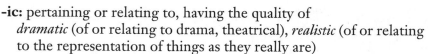
-ic: pertaining or relating to, having the quality of
dramatic (of or relating to drama, theatrical), *realistic* (of or relating to the representation of things as they really are)

-ile: having the qualities of
fragile (easily broken, damaged, or destroyed; frail), *servile* (pertaining to or befitting a slave; abjectly submissive, slavish)

-ish: having the character of
childish (characteristic of, pertaining to, or resembling a child), *foolish* (devoid of good sense or judgment; exhibiting folly, in the manner of a fool)

-ive: performing or tending towards (an action); having the nature of
cooperative (marked by a willingness to cooperate; done with or working with others for a common purpose), *defensive* (serving to defend or protect)

-ous, -ose: full of, having the quality of, relating to
glorious (having or deserving glory, famous), *nauseous* (causing nausea, sickening)

▶ Verb Suffixes

-ate: to make, cause to be or become
deteriorate (to make worse, impair; to make inferior in quality or character), *irritate* (to cause annoyance or disturbance in; to make impatient, angry, annoyed)

-ify, -fy: to make, form into
beautify (to make beautiful), *specify* (to state explicitly or in detail)

-ize: to cause to be or become, to bring about
colonize (to establish a colony), *democratize* (to make or become democratic)

TIPS AND STRATEGIES

A good knowledge of prefixes and suffixes is an invaluable asset when you are building your vocabulary and studying for an exam. Here are some specific tips and strategies to use as you develop this skill and prepare for your test.

- Take the time to memorize the most common prefixes and suffixes. By memorizing these essential word parts, you will be able to learn new words more quickly and better determine the meaning of unfamiliar words.
- Use words that you are very familiar with as examples when you study prefixes and suffixes. The more familiar the word is to you

(e.g., *cooperate*), the easier it will be for you to remember the meaning of the prefix or suffix.

- Remember that you use prefixes and suffixes every day, all the time. Do not feel intimidated by the long lists in this chapter or in Appendix A. You already know much of this material.
- Remember that prefixes and suffixes alone do not create meaning; rather, they change or add to the meaning of the root word. Use as many vocabulary skills as you can to determine meaning, including prefixes and suffixes, word roots (covered in the next two chapters), and context.
- Allow for exceptions. Although most words ending in *-ist* are nouns defining a kind of person (one who does), not every *-ist* word is such a noun. *Elitist* is an example of an adjective with this ending. Check prefixes, word roots, and context if possible to confirm meaning.
- Use your knowledge of prefixes and suffixes to eliminate incorrect answers. The more you narrow down your choices, the better your chances of choosing the correct answer.
- Once you have narrowed down your answer choices, determine the part of speech of each remaining choice. Does it match the part of speech of the definition according to the suffix?
- If you know the prefix or suffix but still aren't sure of meaning, try to recall another word with a similar root. Plug in that meaning with the prefix or suffix and see if it makes sense.

EXTRA HELP

If you would like additional review or further practice with prefixes and suffixes, see Chapters 5 and 6 in LearningExpress's *Vocabulary and Spelling Success in 20 Minutes a Day, 3rd edition.*

PRACTICE

Choose the best answer to each question.

1. *Exorbitant* means:
   a. belonging to a group.
   b. to orbit.
   c. in a new location.
   d. beneath conscious awareness.
   e. far beyond what is normal or reasonable; very high.

2. *Denunciation* means:
   a. to denounce or openly condemn.
   b. critical, of or like a condemnation.
   c. one who denounces or openly condemns another.
   d. the act of denouncing or openly condemning.
   e. to cause to denounce or openly condemn.

3. *Metamorphosis* means:
   a. to transform.
   b. one who has changed.
   c. a transformation.
   d. tending to change frequently.
   e. capable of dramatic change.

4. To *reconcile* means:
   a. to reestablish a close relationship between.
   b. to move away from.
   c. to undermine.
   d. to surpass, outdo.
   e. to put before something else, prioritize.

5. *Didactic* means:
   a. a teacher or instructor.
   b. intended to instruct, moralizing.
   c. to preach, moralize.
   d. the process of instructing.
   e. capable of making moral decisions.

6. *Unilateral* means:
   a. to multiply.
   b. understated.
   c. literal.
   d. one-sided.
   e. a complete equation.

7. *Subordinate* means:
   a. under someone else's authority or control.
   b. organized according to rank, hierarchical.
   c. something ordinary or average, without distinction.
   d. repeated frequently to aid memorization.
   e. unrealistic, highly fantastical.

8. *Incisive* means:
   a. insight.
   b. worthy of consideration.
   c. penetrating, biting in nature.
   d. to act forcefully.
   e. the act of penetrating.

9. *Intermittent* means:
   a. badly handled.
   b. occurring at intervals between two times or points.
   c. greatly varied.
   d. a number between one and ten.
   e. gathered together in defiance or opposition.

10. *Miscreant* means:
    a. someone who is unconventional.
    b. someone who lacks creativity.
    c. a very naãve person.
    d. a newly elected official.
    e. an evil person, villain.

11. *Perennial* means:
    a. lasting a very long time, constant.
    b. one who plants a garden.
    c. to establish contact.
    d. the process of encoding a message.
    e. a person who is trustworthy and dependable.

12. *Imperialism* means:
    a. one who acquires items from other empires.
    b. an empire built by acquiring other territories.
    c. relating to the acquisition of territories.
    d. the policy of extending an empire by acquiring other territories.
    e. to extend an empire by force.

13. To *subjugate* means:
    a. to be the subject of a sentence or conversation.
    b. to conquer, bring under control.
    c. to be wrongly or unevenly distributed.
    d. to be surrounded on all sides.
    e. to drive away from the source.

14. *Benevolence* means:
   a. kindness, generosity.
   b. a kind, generous ruler.
   c. to be generous with one's time or money.
   d. kind, giving charitably.
   e. deserving thanks for one's kindness.

15. To *coalesce* means:
   a. to dig up, mine.
   b. to carry out an ill-conceived or poorly planned course of action.
   c. to combine and form a whole; join together.
   d. to withdraw silently, especially in shame.
   e. to be very small, barely detectable.

16. *Docile* means:
   a. one who domesticates animals.
   b. the management of domestic affairs.
   c. obedience.
   d. willing to obey, easily managed or taught.
   e. to obey authority.

17. *Anomaly* means:
   a. regularity, consistency.
   b. something that is irregular, abnormal, or deviates from the usual form.
   c. a surprising collaboration, the cooperation of unlikely individuals.
   d. discontent among a specific group within a larger population.
   e. excessive greed.

18. *Lamentable* means:
   a. regrettable, unfortunate.
   b. to regret.
   c. an unfortunate occurrence.
   d. to do something regrettable.
   e. one who feels regret.

19. To *abscond* means:
   a. to create a secret hiding place.
   b. to do something without telling anyone.
   c. to go away secretly and hide.
   d. to do something ahead of deadline.
   e. to be opposed to.

20. *Disparate* means:
   a. chosen from within.
   b. exceeding expectations.
   c. from the same origin.
   d. able to move across barriers.
   e. fundamentally different, distinct or apart from others.

21. *Rectify* means:
   a. to correct.
   b. a correction.
   c. a surprising error.
   d. an editor.
   e. erroneous.

22. *Inscrutable* means:
   a. teaching a lesson.
   b. having little or no impact.
   c. kept between or within members of a family.
   d. not fathomable; incapable of being understood.
   e. surrounded by smoke or fog.

23. *Antipathy* means:
   a. that which occurred previously.
   b. a strong aversion or dislike.
   c. an examination of all aspects of an issue.
   d. the act of separating from the source.
   e. an incorrect accusation.

24. *Neophyte* means:
   a. original, unique.
   b. something that comes from multiple sources.
   c. a roommate; someone who lives with another.
   d. a beginner or novice.
   e. a person who refuses to compromise.

25. *Nonchalant* means:
   a. challenging.
   b. done with the intent of harming another.
   c. not showing anxiety or excitement; indifferent.
   d. reversing a previous opinion or decision.
   e. ancient.

ANSWERS

1. e. The prefix *ex-* means out, out of, away from. *Exorbitant* means greatly exceeding (far away from) the bounds of what is normal or reasonable.

2. d. The noun suffix *-tion* means the act or state of. *Denunciation* means the act of denouncing, especially in public; to openly condemn or accuse of evil.

3. c. The noun suffix *-sis* means the process of. *Metamorphosis* means a transformation, a marked change of form, character, or function. Choices **b** and **c** are both nouns, but for choice **b** to be correct, it would require the suffix *-ist*.

4. a. The prefix *re-* means back, again. To *reconcile* means to reestablish a close relationship between, to bring back to harmony.

5. b. The adjective suffix *-ic* means pertaining or relating to, having the quality of. *Didactic* means intended to instruct; tending to be excessively instructive or moralizing. Only choices **b** and **e** define a quality, and choice **e** would require the suffix *-able/ible*.

6. d. The prefix *uni-* means one. *Unilateral* means one-sided. Notice also the adjective suffix *-al*, meaning action or process.

7. a. The prefix *sub-* means under, beneath, below. The adjective *subordinate* means (1) of a lower or inferior class or rank; secondary; (2) subject to the authority or control of another. As a noun it means one that is subordinate to another, and as a verb (notice the *-ate* suffix) it means (1) to put in a lower or inferior rank or class; (2) to make subservient; subdue.

8. c. The adjective suffix *-ive* means having the nature of. *Incisive* means penetrating and clear; sharp, acute, biting.

9. b. The prefix *inter-* means between or among. *Intermittent* means occurring at intervals, not continuous; periodic, alternate.

10. e. The prefix *mis-* means bad, evil, wrong. *Miscreant* means a villain, criminal; an evil person.

11. a. The adjective suffix *-ial* means having the quality of, related to, suitable for. *Perennial* means lasting an indefinitely long time, forever; constantly recurring, happening again and again or year after year. Choice **a** is the only adjective definition.

12. d. The noun suffix *-ism* means state or doctrine of. *Imperialism* means the policy of extending rule of a nation or empire by acquiring other territories.

13. b. The prefix *sub-* means under or below. To *subjugate* means to conquer, subdue, bring under control. Notice also the verb suffix *-ate*, meaning one that performs, promotes, or causes an action; being in a specified state or condition.

14. a. The noun suffix *-ence* means state of. *Benevolence* means the inclination to be kind and generous; a disposition to act charitably.

15. c. The prefix *co-* means with, together. *Coalesce* means to combine and form a whole; to join together, fuse.

16. d. The adjective suffix *-ile* means having the qualities of. *Docile* means willing to obey, reading and willing to be taught, or easily managed.

17. b. The prefix *a-* means not, without. *Anomaly* means something that deviates from the general rule or usual form; one that is irregular or abnormal.

18. a. The adjective suffix *-able* means capable or worthy of. *Lamentable* means regrettable, unfortunate; inspiring grief or mourning.

19. c. The prefix *ab-* means off, away from, apart, down. To *abscond* means to go away secretly and hide oneself, especially after wrongdoing.

20. e. The prefix *dis-* means away from, apart, reversal, not. *Disparate* means fundamentally different or distinct; dissimilar, varied.

21. a. The verb suffix *-ify* means to make. To *rectify* means to make right, correct.

22. d. The prefix *in-* means not. *Inscrutable* means baffling, unfathomable, incapable of being understood. Notice also the adjective suffix *-able*, which means to be capable of.

23. b. The prefix *anti-* means against, opposed to. *Antipathy* means a strong aversion or dislike.

24. d. The prefix *neo-* means new, recent, a new form of. *Neophyte* means a beginner or novice.

25. c. The prefix *non-* means not. *Nonchalant* means indifferent or cool, not showing anxiety or excitement.

WORD LIST

abscond (ab·ˈskond) *v.* to go away secretly and hide oneself, especially after wrongdoing to avoid prosecution.

agrarian (ă·ˈgrair·i·ăn) *adj.* relating to or concerning land and its ownership or cultivation.

anomaly (ă·ˈnom·ă·lee) *n.* something that deviates from the general rule or usual form; one that is irregular, peculiar, or abnormal.

antagonist (an·ˈtag·ŏ·nist) *n.* one who opposes or contends with another; an adversary, opponent.

antecedent (an·ti·ˈsee·děnt) *n.* that which precedes; the thing, circumstance, event that came before.

antipathy (an·ˈtip·ă·thee) *n.* 1. a strong aversion or dislike 2. an object of aversion.

benevolence (bĕ·ˈnev·ŏ·lĕns) *n.* the inclination to be kind and generous; a disposition to act charitably.

circumspect (ˈsur·kŭm·spekt) *adj.* cautious, wary, watchful.

coalesce (koh·ă·les) *v.* to combine and form a whole; to join together, fuse.

consensus (kŏn·ˈsen·sŭs) *n.* general agreement or accord; an opinion or position reached by a group.

denunciation (di·nun·si·ˈay·shŏn) *n.* the act of denouncing, especially in public; to openly condemn or accuse of evil.

didactic (dī·ˈdak·tik) *adj.* 1. intended to instruct 2. tending to be excessively instructive or moralizing.

disparate (ˈdis·pă·rit) *adj.* fundamentally different or distinct; dissimilar, varied.

docile (ˈdos·īl) *adj.* 1. willing to obey, tractable 2. ready and willing to be taught 3. easily managed or handled.

dubious (ˈdoo·bi·ŭs) *adj.* 1. doubtful, questionable 2. fraught with uncertainty, wavering.

embellish (em·'bel·ish) *v.* 1. to make beautiful by adding ornamentation; decorate, adorn 2. to expand a story by adding details that are interesting but often fictitious.

exorbitant (ig·'zor·bi·tănt) *adj.* greatly exceeding the bounds of what is normal or reasonable; inordinate and excessive.

galvanize ('gal·vă·nīz) *v.* 1. to stimulate or rouse into awareness or action 2. to coat with zinc to protect from rust 3. to stimulate by electric shock.

imperialism (im·'peer·i·ă·liz·ĕm) *n.* the policy of extending the rule or authority of a nation or empire by acquiring other territories or dependencies.

incisive (in·'sī·siv) *adj.* penetrating and clear; sharp, acute, biting.

inscrutable (in·'scroo·tă·bĕl) *adj.* baffling, unfathomable, incapable of being understood.

intermittent (in·tĕr·'mit·ĕnt) *adj.* occurring at intervals, not continuous; periodic, alternate.

lamentable ('lam·ĕn·tă·bĕl) *adj.* 1. regrettable, unfortunate; inspiring grief or mourning 2. deplorable, pitiable.

malign (mă·'līn) *v.* to say evil, harmful and often untrue things about someone; to speak evil of.

metamorphosis (met·ă·'mor·fŏ·sis) *n.* a transformation, a marked change of form, character, or function.

miscreant ('mis·kree·ănt) *n.* a villain, criminal; evil person.

multifaceted (mul·tee·'fas·ĕ·tid) *adj.* having many facets or aspects; complex.

neophyte ('nee·ŏ·fīt) *n.* 1. a beginner or novice 2. a recent convert to a belief.

nonchalant (non·shă·lahnt) *adj.* indifferent or cool, not showing anxiety or excitement.

parity ('par·i·tee) *n.* equality in status, amount, value, or degree; equivalence.

perennial (pĕ·'ren·i·ăl) *adj.* 1. lasting an indefinitely long time, forever 2. constantly recurring, happening again and again or year after year 3. of plants, living for more than three years.

polyglot ('pol·i·glot) *n.* one who speaks or understands several languages.

presage ('pres·ij) *v.* to indicate or warn of in advance; to predict, foretell; *n.* an omen, prophesy or warning of a future occurrence; an intuition about what is going to occur.

reconcile ('rek·ŏn·sīl) *v.* 1. to reestablish a close relationship between, especially after a quarrel or estrangement; to bring back to harmony 2. to bring oneself to accept, come to terms with 3. to make compatible or consistent.

rectify ('rek·tĭ·fī) *v.* 1. to set right, correct 2. to purify or refine.

squeamish (′skwee·mish) *adj.* easily sickened, disgusted, nauseated or shocked.

subjugate (′sub·jŭ·gayt) *v.* to conquer, subdue, bring under control or domination; vanquish.

subordinate (sŭ·′bor·dĭ·nit) *adj.* 1. of a lower or inferior class or rank; secondary 2. subject to the authority or control of another; *n.* one that is subordinate to another; (sŭ·′bor·dĭ·nayt) *v.* 1. to put in a lower or inferior rank or class 2. to make subservient; subdue.

supercilious (soo·pĕr·′sil·i·ŭs) *adj.* with an air of superiority; haughty, scornful, disdainful.

unilateral (yoo·nĭ·′lat·ĕ·răl) *adj.* one-sided; performed or undertaken by or affecting only one side, person, group, nation, etc.

venerate (′ven·ĕ·rayt) *v.* to regard with deep respect or reverence; to honor with a sense of awe, revere.

4

Latin Word Roots

Prefixes and suffixes attach to word roots—the base parts of words that typically convey the bulk of their meaning. The more word roots you know, the more you will be able to determine the meaning of unfamiliar words and the better you will understand words you already know. This chapter reviews common Latin word roots. Before you begin learning and reviewing Latin word roots, take a few minutes to take this ten-question *Benchmark Quiz*. These questions are similar to the type of questions that you will find on important tests. When you are finished, check the answer key carefully to assess your results. Your Benchmark Quiz analysis will help you determine how much time you need to spend on this area as well as the specific words you need to learn in order to increase your vocabulary power. A complete list of the vocabulary words used in this lesson is provided at the end of the chapter.

BENCHMARK QUIZ

For each question below, use the Latin word root to determine the meaning of the italicized word.

1. An *amiable* person is:
    a. talkative, loud.
    b. truthful, honest.
    c. highly educated.
    d. friendly, good natured.
    e. full of life, energetic.

2. A *lucid* argument:
    a. is very clear and intelligible.
    b. is loosely held together, tenuous.
    c. frequently digresses.
    d. errs repeatedly in its logic.
    e. assigns blame to others.

3. A *complacent* person:
    a. frequently makes mistakes, but does not accept responsibility.
    b. likes to pick fights.
    c. is contented to a fault, self-satisfied.
    d. is known to tell lies, embellish the truth.
    e. is full of life, vivacious.

4. To *exacerbate* a problem means:
    a. to solve it.
    b. to analyze it.
    c. to lessen it.
    d. to worsen it.
    e. to ignore it.

5. To measure the *veracity* of something is to measure its:
    a. value or worth.
    b. truthfulness.
    c. weight.
    d. circumference.
    e. life force.

6. Something that is *eloquent* is:
   a. dull, trite, hackneyed.
   b. expressed in a powerful and effective manner.
   c. very old, antiquated.
   d. not fit for consumption, inedible.
   e. equally divided or apportioned.

7. To *indict* someone is to:
   a. pick a fight with that person.
   b. stop or block that person from doing something.
   c. harm that person.
   d. charge that person with a crime.
   e. love that person dearly.

8. A *quiescent* place is:
   a. very isolated.
   b. tumultuous, chaotic.
   c. harmful, dangerous.
   d. sacred.
   e. still, at rest.

9. A *noxious* odor is:
   a. harmful.
   b. unscented.
   c. tantalizing.
   d. refreshing.
   e. nostalgic.

10. A person with *equanimity:*
    a. has a violent temper.
    b. is very stubborn.
    c. enjoys the company of others.
    d. is even-tempered and composed.
    e. is guilty of wrongdoing.

BENCHMARK QUIZ SOLUTIONS

How did you do on identifying Latin word roots? Check your answers here, and then analyze the results to figure out your plan of attack for mastering this topic.

▶ *Answers*

1. **d.** The root *am* means love. *Amiable* means friendly and agreeable; good natured, likeable, pleasing.

2. **a.** The root *luc/lum/lus* means light. *Lucid* means very clear, easy to understand, intelligible.

3. **c.** The root *plac* means to please. *Complacent* means contented to a fault; self-satisfied (pleased with oneself).

4. **d.** The root *ac* means sharp, bitter. To *exacerbate* means to make worse; to increase the severity, violence, or bitterness of.

5. **b.** The root *ver* means truth. *Veracity* means truth, truthfulness.

6. **b.** The root *loc/log/loqu* means word, speech. *Eloquent* means expressed in a powerful, fluent, and persuasive manner.

7. **d.** The root *dic/dict/dit* means to say, tell, use words. To *indict* means to formally accuse of or charge with a crime.

8. **e.** The root *qui* means quiet. *Quiescent* means inactive, quiet, at rest.

9. **a.** The root *nec/nic/noc/nox* means harm, death. *Noxious* means unpleasant and harmful, unwholesome.

10. **d.** The root *equ* means equal, even. *Equanimity* means calmness of temperament, even-temperedness; patience and composure, especially under stress.

BENCHMARK QUIZ RESULTS

If you answered 8–10 questions correctly, well done! You are already skilled at using Latin word roots to determining meaning. Give the lesson a quick review and do the practice exercise. If your score on the practice test is equally high, move on to Chapter 5.

If you answered 4–7 questions correctly, you are familiar with some of the most common Latin word roots and how to use them to determine meaning. But you need more practice to really sharpen this skill. Be sure to set aside some time to carefully review the complete list of common Latin word roots located in Appendix A.

If you answered 1–3 questions correctly, perhaps it has been some time since you reviewed word roots. Study the lesson that follows carefully, and do the practice quiz on a separate sheet of paper so that you can do the exercise several times if necessary. Take extra time to learn the complete list of common Latin word roots located in Appendix A.

JUST IN TIME LESSON—LATIN WORD ROOTS

Just as many Americans have their roots in other countries, so, too, do many of the words in the English language. In fact, most English words have been borrowed from other languages throughout the centuries, and it is composed largely of words built upon root words from other cultures. The two most important categories of roots to learn are Latin and Greek because so many English words are built upon Latin and Greek word bases. For example, *manual* and *manufacture* share the Latin root *man*, meaning hand; *anonymous* and *synonym* share the Greek root *nom/nym*, meaning name.

Needless to say, the more roots you know, the stronger your vocabulary will be. As you break down unfamiliar words into their parts, you will be more likely to recognize the roots and therefore more accurately determine meaning. You will also have a better understanding of the words you already know.

GLOSSARY

ETYMOLOGY the history of a word, the study of its origin and development

On occasion, Latin and Greek roots are themselves words. The Latin roots *err* and *pug*, for example, are English words as well, meaning to make a mistake and a boxer, respectively. But most of the time, roots are the base to which prefixes and suffixes (and sometimes other roots) are attached to create a rich variety of meaning. Take, for example, the Latin root *ced/ceed/cess*, meaning to go, yield, stop. Notice how many different words can be created by adding different prefixes and suffixes to this root and how the different prefixes and suffixes change meaning:

ante**ced**ent: that which precedes or comes before
cessation: a stopping, a bringing to an end
con**cede**: to acknowledge or admit as true, proper, etc. (often with reluctance); to yield, surrender
con**cess**ion: the act of conceding or yielding; a thing yielded, an acknowledgement or admission
ex**ceed**: to extend beyond or outside of; surpass
pre**cede**: to come or go before in time, place, rank, or importance
prede**cess**or: one who precedes or comes before another in time (as in holding an office or position)

pro**ceed**: to go forward or onward, especially after an interruption; move on, advance

pro**ced**ure: the act or manner of proceeding; a course of action or conduct; process

Thus, *recede* means:

    a. to go forward blindly.
    b. to stop or abandon before completion.
    c. to move or go back, retreat.
    d. to go together with others.
    e. to yield to the decision of a superior.

Remember your prefixes from Chapter 3. *Re-* means back, again; *ced* means to go, yield, stop. *Recede* means **c**, to move back, withdraw, retreat. Now add the noun suffix *-sion*, meaning the act or state of, and you get:

recession: the act of withdrawing or going back

With your knowledge of prefixes and suffixes, you can also answer this question:

Incessant means:
    a. traveling to many places or locations, itinerant.
    b. not stopping, continuing without interruption.
    c. to move or go below the surface, subliminal.
    d. going between, through, or among; not direct.
    e. yielding readily under pressure.

The correct answer is **b**. The prefix *in-* means not; *cess* means to go, stop, or yield; and the suffix *-ant* means being in a state or condition of; performing or causing an action. Thus, *incessant* means continuing without interruption; ceaseless, continuous.

Here are several words formed from another Latin root, *plac*, meaning to please. Again, notice the rich variety of meaning created by adding different prefixes and suffixes to the root word:

placate: to appease, pacify; to allay the anger of, especially by making concessions

im**plac**able: incapable of being placated or appeased; inexorable

placid: calm and peaceful; free from disturbance or tumult

com**plac**ent: contented to a fault; self-satisfied, unconcerned

placebo: an inactive, harmless substance of no medicinal value given to patients to reassure them or to members of a control group in experiments testing the efficacy of a drug

SHORTCUT: MAKE THE MOST OF YOUR LEARNING STYLE

For many people, especially visual learners, the best way to memorize words is to create a picture in the mind associated with that word. For example, to remember the root *pug*, you might picture a pug dog in a boxing ring, or a boxer with a pug nose. Similarly, you might picture a stop sign with the root *ced* written on it instead of *stop*, or a yield sign with *cess* instead of *yield*. You could also picture a traffic light for the root *ced/ceed/cess*, since the colors of the traffic light correspond with the three meanings of this root: go, stop, yield.

If you are an auditory learner, you can come up with rhymes or short sentences to help you remember root meanings. For example, you could try one of these sentences for the root *am*, meaning love:

> I *am* love.
> I love *Am*y.
> I love h*am*.

Below is a list of some of the most common Latin word roots. You have already seen some of these roots in the words from the Benchmark Quiz and this lesson. Review the list carefully, taking note of the examples, which once again are mostly everyday words that are already part of your permanent vocabulary. A more comprehensive list of the most common Latin and Greek word roots is located in Appendix A. After you have completed this lesson, make sure you review the list carefully and study any roots that are unfamiliar to you.

COMMON LATIN WORD ROOTS

ac, acr: sharp, bitter
  acid (something that is sharp, sour, or ill natured), *acute* (extremely sharp or severe; keenly perceptive)
am: love
  amorous (inclined to love; romantic, affectionate), *enamored* (inflamed or inspired by love; captivated)
bel: war
  antebellum (before the war, especially the American Civil War), *rebel* (to resist or defy authority)
cast, chast: cut
  caste (a social class separated from others by hereditary rank, profession, etc.), *chastise* (to punish severely, as with a beating; to rebuke)

ced, ceed, cess: to go, yield, stop
antecedent (that which precedes), *exceed* (to extend beyond or outside of; surpass)

culp: blame
culprit (person accused or guilty of a crime), *mea culpa* (Latin, "my fault")

dic, dict, dit: to say, tell, use words
dictate (to say or read aloud; to issue orders or commands), *predict* (to foretell, make known in advance)

equ: equal, even
equate (to make or consider two things as equal), *equidistant* (equally distant)

err: to wander
err (to make a mistake), *error* (a mistake; an incorrect or wrong action)

ferv: to boil, bubble, burn
fervid (very hot, burning; ardent, vehement), *effervescent* (bubbling up, as a carbonated liquid; high spirited, animated)

loc, log, loqu: word, speech
dialogue (a conversation between two or more people), *neologism* (a new word or phrase)

luc, lum, lus: light
illuminate (to brighten with light; enlighten), *translucent* (almost transparent; allowing light to pass through diffusely)

lug, lut, luv: to wash
dilute (to make thinner or weaker by adding a liquid such as water; to lessen the force or purity of), *pollute* (to make impure or unclean; to make unfit or harmful to living things)

mag, maj, max: big
magnify (to increase in size, volume or significance; to amplify), *maximum* (the greatest possible quantity or degree)

man: hand
manual (operated by hand), *manufacture* (to make by hand or machinery)

min: to project, hang over
prominent (standing out, conspicuous; projecting or jutting beyond the line or surface), *eminent* (towering above or more prominent that others; lofty, distinguished)

nas, nat, nai: to be born
native (a person born in a particular country), *innate* (possessed at birth; inborn, inherent)

nec, nic, noc, nox: harm, death
innocent (uncorrupted by evil; free from guilt; not dangerous or harmful), *obnoxious* (offensive, hateful)

omni: all
omnipresent (everywhere at once), *omnipotent* (all powerful)

plac: to please
> *placid* (calm and peaceful), *placate* (to appease or pacify)

pon, pos, pound: to put, place
> *deposit* (to put or set down; place), *transpose* (to reverse or transfer the order or place of; interchange)

pug: to fight
> *pug* (a boxer), *repugnant* (highly offensive or distasteful; hostile, disposed to fight)

qui: quiet
> *quiet* (making little or no noise; calm, still), *tranquil* (free from disturbance, anxiety, or tension)

rog: to ask
> *interrogate* (to examine by asking a series of questions), *prerogative* (an exclusive privilege or right belonging to a person or group)

sci: to know
> *conscious* (knowing and perceiving, aware), *science* (knowledge, especially that gained through systematic study)

tac, tic: to be silent
> *tacit* (not spoken; implied), *taciturn* (habitually untalkative, reserved)

ver: truth
> *verdict* (the findings of a jury in a trial; decision or judgment), *verify* (to confirm the truth of)

vi: life
> *vivid* (evoking life-like images in the mind; true to life; bright, brilliant, distinct), *vigorous* (energetic, forceful, active, strong)

voc, vok: to call
> *vocal* (of or pertaining to the voice; tending to express oneself often and freely, outspoken), *revoke* (to cancel, call back, reverse, withdraw)

CHEAT SHEET: THE POWER OF ASSOCIATION

Need more help memorizing word roots? Use the power of association. A rebel, for example, fights in a war; the meaning of the root bel is war. The acute pain you felt in your ankle when you sprained it was very sharp; the root ac means sharp, bitter.

Similarly, as you are learning roots and trying to determine the meaning of unfamiliar words, especially on an exam, think of other words that sound like they might share a root word. For example, if you don't know the meaning of amiable but you do know what enamored means, you can at least determine that amiable is probably a positive thing and that it probably has something to do with love or friendship.

Now you have the tools to really break down words and work out their meanings. By memorizing common prefixes, suffixes, and word roots, you will be able to accurately guess the meaning of many unfamiliar words, and this will both dramatically expand your vocabulary and significantly improve your score on your exam.

EXTRA HELP

If you would like additional review or further practice with word roots, see Lessons 7 and 8 in LearningExpress's *Vocabulary and Spelling Success in 20 Minutes a Day, 3rd edition*.

TIPS AND STRATEGIES

When you are faced with an unfamiliar word in your reading or on an exam, your best strategy is to break it down into its parts and look for a familiar word root. Here are some specific strategies for sharpening this skill and using it in a test situation.

- Take the time to memorize as many Latin roots as you can. There are more words built upon Latin roots than any other in the English language. By memorizing these word bases, you will be able to learn new words more quickly and better determine the meaning of unfamiliar words.
- Use words that you are very familiar with as examples when you study word roots. The more familiar the word is to you (e.g., *predict, equate*), the easier it will be for you to remember the meaning of the root word. Use words that create a vivid picture in your imagination.
- Remember that you use common word roots every day, often without realizing it. Do not feel intimidated by the long lists in this chapter or in Appendix A. You already know much of this material.
- Remember that word roots work with prefixes and suffixes—and sometimes other root words—to create meaning. Look at all parts of the word and the context, if possible, to determine meaning.
- Remember the power of elimination on an exam. Use your knowledge of word roots to eliminate incorrect answers. The more you narrow down your choices, the better your chances of choosing the correct answer.
- Use the power of association. If you don't know or can't remember the root word, try to recall the meaning of another word with a similar root.

PRACTICE

Choose the best answer for each question below.

1. A *belligerent* person is:
   a. from another country, foreign.
   b. kind, eager to help.
   c. eager to fight, hostile.
   d. loving, devoted.
   e. bitter and angry.

2. Someone who is *omniscient:*
   a. often speaks without thinking.
   b. receives the maximum benefit.
   c. blames others for his or her own faults.
   d. is eager to please.
   e. is all-knowing.

3. A *renaissance* is:
   a. a rebirth.
   b. a punishment.
   c. a lie.
   d. a mistake.
   e. a speech.

4. To *equivocate* is to:
   a. burn or sting.
   b. speak in a way that conceals the truth.
   c. put something in its proper place.
   d. calm or quiet.
   e. cause harm or damage to, especially by accident.

5. Something that is *manifest* is:
   a. everywhere.
   b. newborn.
   c. obvious.
   d. deadly.
   e. large.

6. Something that is *luminous* is:
  a. bright, shining.
  b. even, equal.
  c. excessive.
  d. full of knowledge.
  e. silent.

7. A person who is *culpable* is:
  a. capable.
  b. vocal.
  c. energetic, full of life.
  d. burning with anger.
  e. guilty.

8. Something that is *innocuous* is:
  a. dangerous or deadly.
  b. irrelevant, wandering from the main path or point.
  c. harmless, inoffensive.
  d. clean, thoroughly washed.
  e. projecting over the edge.

9. To *juxtapose* is to:
  a. place side by side.
  b. overwhelm, flood.
  c. be born again.
  d. speak in a round-about manner.
  e. wash away, erode.

10. Someone who is *reticent* is:
  a. fair, judging equally.
  b. reserved, silent.
  c. bubbling over with enthusiasm.
  d. deeply in love.
  e. a great warrior.

11. A *veritable* autograph is:
  a. very valuable.
  b. an autograph by a famous person.
  c. genuine.
  d. a forgery or fake.
  e. worthless.

12. To *abrogate* is to:
  a. abolish, revoke.
  b. fight, quarrel.
  c. rest quietly.
  d. know intimately.
  e. witness silently.

13. An *acrimonious* relationship is one that:
  a. has existed for a long time.
  b. is extremely friendly.
  c. exists only in the imagination.
  d. is bitter or resentful.
  e. is enlightened.

14. A *vicarious* action is one that:
  a. is experienced through the life or action of another.
  b. enables a guilty person to be set free.
  c. surrenders the rights of others.
  d. has a pleasing and lasting affect on others.
  e. is of great importance.

15. If there is *amity* between two nations, there is:
  a. war.
  b. equality.
  c. bitterness.
  d. trading of blame.
  e. friendship.

16. An *edict* is:
  a. a place to rest.
  b. a place to stop.
  c. the act of seeing or shining.
  d. a formal proclamation or command.
  e. a state of danger or peril.

17. A *magnanimous* person is:
  a. highly noble, generous.
  b. extremely talkative.
  c. given to wordy, rambling speech.
  d. a wanderer, hobo.
  e. someone with a sharp wit, sarcastic.

18. To *acquiesce* is to:
   a. to call attention to.
   b. to speak in a whisper.
   c. to mask the truth.
   d. to give in to, comply with another's wishes.
   e. to wish to live another's life, to want to be someone else.

19. A *pugnacious* person is best described as:
   a. nosy.
   b. combative.
   c. talented.
   d. ruthless.
   e. evil.

20. Something that is *erratic:*
   a. moves at a constant, steady pace.
   b. is properly ordered; appropriate, in its proper place.
   c. seems to be harmless but is actually very dangerous.
   d. is cut or divided into equal parts.
   e. is unpredictable, meandering, straying from the norm.

21. To feel *fervor* is to feel:
   a. carefree, light-hearted.
   b. burdened, as with guilt.
   c. intense, fiery emotion.
   d. calmness, peace.
   e. an inability to express oneself.

22. A *loquacious* person:
   a. has good intentions, but often ends up doing things that end up hurting others.
   b. tends to talk a great deal.
   c. often has difficulty finding things.
   d. tends to like everyone; is not discerning.
   e. believes in doing what pleases him or herself.

23. To *castigate* means to:
   a. pick a fight with, tease.
   b. disturb the peace.
   c. verbally abuse, cut down; punish harshly.
   d. to expand to so great a size as to outgrow; balloon, distend.
   e. to accept blame for another's wrongdoing.

24. A *deluge* is:
  a. a mask, something hidden.
  b. a skillfully-told lie.
  c. an aggressive or hostile person.
  d. a flood, an overwhelming amount.
  e. a decree abolishing something, a revocation.

25. Something that is *preeminent:*
  a. stands out above or surpasses others.
  b. is related to a specific branch of scientific knowledge.
  c. reflects the opinions, feelings, etc. of everyone within the group.
  d. is handled carefully and tactfully; diplomatic.
  e. is easily permeated by water.

ANSWERS

1. c. The root *bel* means war. The adjective suffix *-ent* means in a state or condition; performing or causing a specified action. *Belligerent* means hostile and aggressive, showing an eagerness to fight.

2. e. The root *omni* means all; the root *sci* means to know. *Omniscient* means having infinite knowledge, knowing all things.

3. a. The root *nas/nat/nai* means to be born. The prefix *re-* means back or again; the suffix *-ance* means state of. *Renaissance* means a rebirth or revival.

4. b. The root *equ* means equal; the root *voc/vok* means to call; the suffix *-ate* means to make, cause to be. To *equivocate* means to use unclear or ambiguous language in order to mislead or conceal the truth. Thus, someone who equivocates is "equally" lying and telling the truth (or rather, not quite doing either).

5. c. The root *man* means hand. *Manifest* means clear and unmistakable, obvious; thus, at hand. The correct answer can be achieved here through the process of elimination, as the other answers correspond with different roots.

6. a. The root *luc/lum/lus* means light; the suffix *-ous* means having the quality of or relating to. *Luminous* means shining, emitting light; full of light, brilliant.

7. e. The root *culp* means blame. The adjective suffix *-able* means capable or worthy of. *Culpable* means deserving blame or censure for doing something wrong or harmful; blameworthy, guilty.

8. a. The root *nec/nic/noc/nox* means harm, death. The prefix *in-* means not; the suffix *-ous* means having the quality of or relating to. Thus, *innocuous* means harmless, having no adverse or ill effects.

9. a. The root *pon/pos/pound* means to put, place. To *juxtapose* means to place side by side, especially to compare or contrast.

10. b. The root *tac/tic* means to be silent. *Reticent* means tending to keep one's thoughts and feelings to oneself; reserved, untalkative, silent.

11. c. The root *ver* means truth. The suffix *-able* means capable or worthy of. *Veritable* means real, true, genuine.

12. a. The root *rog* means to ask. The prefix *ab-* means off, away from, away, down; the suffix *-ate* means to make, cause to be. To *abrogate* means to abolish, do away with, formally revoke.

13. d. The root *ac/acr* means sharp, bitter. The adjective suffix *-ous* means having the quality of or relating to. *Acrimonious* means bitter and sharp in language or tone.

14. a. The root *vi* means life. The adjective suffix *-ous* means having the quality of or relating to. *Vicarious* means felt through imaging what another has experienced; acting or suffering for another.

15. e. The root *am* means love. The noun suffix *-ity* means state of being. *Amity* means friendship; a state of friendly or peaceful relations.

16. d. The root *dic/dict/dit* means to say, tell, use words. An *edict* is an official order or decree; a formal proclamation or command issued by someone in authority.

17. a. The root *mag/maj/max* means big. The adjective suffix *-ous* means having the quality of or relating to. *Magnanimous* means very noble and generous; understanding and forgiving of others.

18. d. The root *qui* means quiet. To *acquiesce* means to comply, give in, consent without protest—thereby "quieting" the other to whom one gives in.

19. b. The root *pug* means to fight. The adjective suffix *-ous* means having the quality of or relating to. *Pugnacious* means quarrelsome, combative, inclined to fight.

20. e. The root *err* means to wander. The adjective suffix *-ic* means pertaining or relating to, having the quality of. *Erratic* means moving or behaving in an irregular, uneven, or inconsistent manner; deviating (wandering) from the normal or typical course of action, opinion, etc.

21. c. The root *ferv* means to boil, bubble, burn. The suffix *-or* means a condition or activity. *Fervor* means zeal, ardor, intense emotion.

22. b. The root *loc/log/loqu* means word, speech. The adjective suffix *-ous* means having the quality of or relating to. *Loquacious* means very talkative, garrulous.

23. c. The root *cast/chast* means cut. The verb suffix *-ate* means to make, cause to be. To *castigate* means to inflict a severe punishment on; to chastise (verbally abuse, cut down) severely.

24. d. The root *lug/lut/luv* means to wash. A *deluge* is a great flood or inundation; something that overwhelms, an overwhelming number or amount.

25. a. The root *min* means to project, hang over. The prefix *pre-* means before; the suffix *-ent* means in a state or condition; performing or causing a specified action. *Preeminent* means greater to others in importance, degree, significance, or achievement; superior, surpassing—thus, coming before, standing above others in its class.

WORD LIST

abrogate ('ab·rŏ·gayt) *v.* to abolish, do away with, formally revoke.

acquiesce (ak·wi·'es) *v.* to comply, give in, consent without protest.

acrimonious (ak·rĭ·'moh·ni·ŭs) *adj.* bitter and sharp in language or tone.

amiable ('ay·mi·ă·bĕl) *adj.* friendly and agreeable; good natured, likable, pleasing.

amity ('am·ĭ·tee) *n.* friendship; a state of friendly or peaceful relations.

belligerent (bi·'lij·ĕr·ĕnt) *adj.* hostile and aggressive, showing an eagerness to fight.

castigate ('kas·tĭ·gayt) *v.* to inflict a severe punishment on; to chastise severely.

complacent (kŏm·'play·sĕnt) *adj.* contented to a fault; self·satisfied, unconcerned.

concede (kŏn·'seed) *v.* 1. to acknowledge or admit as true, proper, etc. (often with reluctance); to yield, surrender 2. to grant as a right or privilege.

culpable ('kul·pă·bĕl) *adj.* deserving blame or censure for being or doing something wrong or harmful; blameworthy, guilty.

deluge ('del·yooj) *n.* 1. a great flood or inundation 2. something that overwhelms, an overwhelming number or amount; *v.* 1. to overrun with water, inundate 2. to overwhelm with a large number or amount, swamp.

edict ('ee·dikt) *n.* an official order or decree; a formal proclamation or command issued by someone in authority.

eloquent ('el·ŏ·kwĕnt) *adj.* expressed in a powerful, fluent, and persuasive manner; clear, vivid, and effective expression.

equanimity (ee·kwă·'nim·i·tee) *n.* calmness of temperament, even-temperedness; patience and composure, especially under stressful circumstances.

equivocate (i·'kwiv·ŏ·kayt) *v.* to use unclear or ambiguous language in order to mislead or conceal the truth.

erratic (i·'rat·ik) *adj.* 1. moving or behaving in an irregular, uneven, or inconsistent manner 2. deviating from the normal or typical course of action, opinion, etc.

exacerbate (ig·'zas·ĕr·bayt) *v.* to make worse; to increase the severity, violence, or bitterness of.

fervor ('fur·vŏr) *n.* zeal, ardor, intense emotion.

implacable (im·'plak·ă·bĕl) *adj.* incapable of being placated or appeased; inexorable.

incessant (in·'ses·ănt) *adj.* continuing without interruption; ceaseless, continuous.

indict (in·'dīt) *v.* to formally accuse of or charge with a crime.

innocuous (i·'nok·yoo·ŭs) *adj.* harmless, having no adverse or ill effects; not likely to upset or offend.

juxtapose (juk·stă·'pohz) *v.* to place side by side, especially to compare or contrast.

loquacious (loh·'kway·shŭs) *adj.* very talkative, garrulous.

lucid ('loo·sid) *adj.* 1. very clear, easy to understand, intelligible 2. sane or rational.

luminous ('loo·mĭ·nŭs) *adj.* shining, emitting light; full of light, bright, brilliant.

magnanimous (mag·'nan·ŭ·mŭs) *adj.* very noble and generous; understanding and forgiving of others.

manifest ('man·ĭ·fest) *adj.* clear and unmistakable; obvious; *v.* to show or demonstrate clearly; to become apparent and visible.

noxious ('nok·shŭs) *adj.* unpleasant and harmful, unwholesome.

omniscient (om·'nish·ĕnt) *adj.* having infinite knowledge; knowing all things.

placate ('play·kayt) *v.* to appease, pacify; to allay the anger of, especially by making concessions.

placebo (plă·'see·boh) *n.* an inactive, harmless substance of no medicinal value given to patients to reassure them or to members of a control group in experiments testing the efficacy of a drug.

placid ('plas·id) *adj.* calm and peaceful; free from disturbance or tumult.

preeminent (pree·'em·i·nĕnt) *adj.* greater to others in importance, degree, significance, or achievement; superior, surpassing.

pugnacious (pug·'nay·shŭs) *adj.* quarrelsome, combative, inclined to fight.

quiescent (kwi·'es·ĕnt) *adj.* inactive, quiet, at rest; dormant, latent.

renaissance, renascence (ri·'nas·ĕns, ri·'nay·sĕns) *n.* a rebirth or revival.

reticent ('ret·i·sĕnt) *adj.* tending to keep one's thoughts and feelings to oneself; reserved, untalkative, silent.

veracity (vĕ·'ras·i·tee) *n.* truth, truthfulness.

veritable ('ver·i·tă·bĕl) *adj.* real, true, genuine.

vicarious (vī·'kair·i·ŭs) *adj.* 1. felt through imagining what another has experienced 2. acting or suffering for another.

5

Greek Word Roots

This chapter builds on your knowledge of word roots by reviewing some of the most common roots from the Greek language. Before you begin learning and reviewing Greek word roots, take a few minutes to take this ten-question *Benchmark Quiz*. These questions are similar to the type of questions that you will find on important tests. When you are finished, check the answer key carefully to assess your results. Your Benchmark Quiz analysis will help you determine how much time you need to spend on this area as well as the specific words you need to learn in order to increase your vocabulary power. A complete list of the vocabulary words used in this lesson is provided at the end of the chapter.

BENCHMARK QUIZ

Choose the best answer to each question.

   1. To have *autonomy* means:
     a. to have a great deal of wealth.
     b. to be independent, self-governing.
     c. to be very brave, courageous.
     d. to have very strong opinions.
     e. to have the ability to feel what others feel.

2. *Empathy* means:
   a. doing good for others.
   b. having a great love for others.
   c. being the same as everyone else.
   d. identifying with another's feelings.
   e. being an overachiever, obsessed with success.

3. A state of *euphoria* is:
   a. a state of happiness, bliss.
   b. a state of total control by an absolute ruler.
   c. a state of self-denial.
   d. a state of timelessness, suspension.
   e. a state of disbelief.

4. Something that is *peripheral* is:
   a. central.
   b. a matter of opinion.
   c. dissecting, cutting in two.
   d. secret, hidden.
   e. on the outer edge or boundary.

5. A *pseudonym* is:
   a. a false name.
   b. a god or deity.
   c. a harsh sound.
   d. a long-lasting illness.
   e. an excessively long and critical speech.

6. In a state of *anarchy*, there is:
   a. great suffering.
   b. a strong emphasis on education.
   c. total lawlessness.
   d. great respect for the individual.
   e. the worship of only one god.

7. Something that is *amorphous:*
   a. has no definite shape.
   b. is unable to speak or communicate.
   c. without love or compassion.
   d. has no name.
   e. has a strong resemblance to another.

8. A person who is *dogmatic:*
   a. has a distorted sense of realty.
   b. is unable to tolerate those who are different.
   c. asserts his or her opinion in an absolute, arrogant manner.
   d. has difficulty handling situations in which he or she must lead others.
   e. is secretive, shrouded in mystery.

9. A state of *pandemonium* is:
   a. calm, quiet.
   b. ruled by consensus.
   c. all-encompassing, complete.
   d. noisy and chaotic.
   e. inspirational, generating hope.

10. *Philanthropy* is:
    a. the love of humankind.
    b. a tendency toward or preference for something.
    c. a widespread rumor.
    d. the use of force to rule or control others.
    e. the end of innocence after witnessing or experiencing evil.

BENCHMARK QUIZ SOLUTIONS

How did you do on identifying Greek word roots? Check your answers here, and then analyze the results to figure out your plan of attack for mastering this topic.

▶ *Answers*

1. b. The root *auto* means self. *Autonomy* means personal or political independence; self-government, self-determination.

2. d. The root *pas/pat/path* means feeling, suffering, disease. *Empathy* means understanding and identifying with another's feelings, situation, or motives.

3. a. The root *eu* means good, well. The noun suffix *-ia* identifies names or diseases. *Euphoria* means a feeling of well-being or high spirits.

4. e. The root *peri* means around. The adjective suffix *-al* means of or relating to. *Peripheral* means of or relating to the periphery or edge, on the outer boundary; not of central importance or relevance.

5. a. The Greek root *pseudo* means false, fake. The root *nom/nym* means name. A *pseudonym* is a fictitious name, especially a pen name used by a writer.

6. c. The prefix *a-* means not, without. The root *arch/archi/archy* means chief, principal, ruler. *Anarchy* means the complete absence of government or control resulting in lawlessness; political disorder and confusion.

7. a. The prefix *a-* means not, without. The root *morph* means shape. The adjective suffix *-ous* means having the quality of or relating to. *Amorphous* means having no definite form or distinct shape, shapeless; of no particular kind or character, anomalous.

8. c. The root *dog/dox* means opinion. The adjective suffix *-ic* means pertaining or relating to, having the quality of. *Dogmatic* means asserting something in a positive, absolute, arrogant way; of or relating to dogma.

9. d. The root *pan* means all, everyone; the root *dem* means people. *Pandemonium* means a state of extreme disorder or chaos; a wild uproar, noisy confusion.

10. a. The root *phil* means love; the root *anthro/andro* means man, human. *Philanthropy* means love of humankind; voluntary action intended to promote the welfare of others, or an institution dedicated to this.

BENCHMARK QUIZ RESULTS

If you answered 8–10 questions correctly, well done! You are already skilled at using Greek word roots to determining meaning. Give the lesson a quick review and do the practice exercise. If your score on the practice test is equally high, move on to Chapter 6.

If you answered 4–7 questions correctly, you are familiar with some of the most common Greek word roots and how to use them to determine meaning. But you need more practice to really sharpen this skill. Be sure to set aside some time to carefully review the complete list of common Greek word roots located in Appendix A.

If you answered 1–3 questions correctly, perhaps it has been some time since you reviewed word roots. Study the lesson that follows carefully, and do the practice quiz on a separate sheet of paper so that you can do the exercise several times if necessary. Take extra time to learn the complete list of common Greek word roots located in Appendix A.

JUST IN TIME LESSON—GREEK WORD ROOTS

Just as you can better understand a person by learning about that person's past, you can also better understand words and more effectively build your vocabulary by learning about the history of words. The study of word origins and development is called **etymology**. When you break down a word and identify a root word from another language, you are tracing the etymology or history of that word.

GLOSSARY

ETYMOLOGY the history of a word, the study of its origin and development

Many words have a rich history, and a detailed etymological study will show you not only where a word comes from but also how its meaning has changed over time. For now, however, the focus of this lesson remains on learning some of the most common roots so that you can better determine meaning and succeed on your exam.

Greek word roots work in exactly the same way as Latin roots; they are the bases to which we add prefixes, suffixes, and sometimes other roots to change and create meaning. For example, look at the etymology of the word *homogeneous*:

homo:	Greek root meaning *same*
gen:	Latin root meaning *birth*, *kind*
ous:	suffix meaning *having the quality of, related to*

Thus, *homogeneous* (also spelled *homogenous*) means of the *same* or similar nature or *kind*; having a uniform structure or composition throughout.

As you know from Chapter 4, many different words can be built from a single root. For example, look at the number of words and the rich variety of meaning that comes from the Greek root *chron*, meaning time:

chronic: continuing for a long time; on-going, habitual; long-lasting or recurrent

chronology: the arrangement of events in time; the sequence in which events occurred

chronicle: a detailed record or narrative description of past events; to record in chronological order, make a historical record

chronological: relating to chronology; arranged in order of time of occurrence

chronometer: an exceptionally accurate clock; a precise instrument for measuring time

syn**chron**ize: to cause to occur at the same time or agree in time; to occur at the same time, be simultaneous

By changing the suffix of *synchronize*, we can create even more words. For example, we can turn it into the noun *synchronicity*, which is the state or fact of being *synchronous*, an adjective that means occurring or existing at the same time.

Now use your knowledge of prefixes, suffixes, and roots to answer the following question:

> An *anachronism* is:
> **a.** two people born at the same time.
> **b.** something that is out of date or placed in the wrong time period.
> **c.** the quality of being timely or punctual.
> **d.** someone who has too much time on his or her hands.
> **e.** a temporary state of confusion or disorder.

The correct answer is **b**. The prefix *a-* means not, without, so you know that the definition should somehow express something negative or a lack of something. This effectively eliminates choices **a**, **c**, and **d**. The root *chron*, of course, means time; this rules out choice **e**, which has nothing to do with time. The suffix *-ism* means a state or doctrine of, thus doubly eliminating choices **a**, **c**, and **d**. Thus, an *anachronism* is something that is placed into an incorrect historical period; a person, custom, or idea that is out of date.

Here is a list of some of the most common Greek word roots. You have already seen some of these roots in the words from the Benchmark Quiz and the lesson thus far. Review the list carefully, taking note of the examples, which once again are mostly everyday words that are already part of your permanent vocabulary. A more comprehensive list of the most common Latin and Greek word roots is located in Appendix A. After you have completed this lesson, make sure you review the list carefully and study any roots that are unfamiliar to you.

COMMON GREEK WORD ROOTS

anthro, andro: man, human
android (a very human-like machine or robot, especially one made of biological materials), *anthropology* (the social science that studies the origins and social relationships of human beings)

arch, archi, archy: chief, principal, ruler
architect (one who plans or devises; one who creates plans for buildings), *monarchy* (a state ruled by a monarch (a sole and absolute ruler, such as a king)

auto: self
automatic (operating without external influence or control; having inherent power of action or motion), *autopsy* (examination of a dead body to determine cause of death; seeing with one's own eyes)

card, cord, cour: heart
cardiac (of or relating to the heart), *encourage* (to inspire with hope, courage, or confidence; to give support, hearten)

chron: time
chronic (continuing for a long time; on-going, habitual; long-lasting or recurrent), *chronology* (the arrangement of events in time; the sequence in which events occurred)

cli, clin: to lean toward, bend
incline (to lean, slant, slope, or cause to do so; to have a tendency or disposition toward something), *recline* (to lie back or down)

cryp: hidden
crypt (an underground vault or chamber, especially one used as a burial place), *cryptography* (secret writing; the process or skill of communicating in or deciphering coded messages)

dem: people
democracy (government by the people through elected representatives), *epidemic* (a widespread outbreak of a disease affecting many people at the same time)

di, dia: apart, through
diameter (a straight line passing through the center of a circle; thickness, width), *digress* (to turn aside, deviate, or swerve; to stray from the main subject in writing or speaking)

dog, dox: opinion
dogged (stubbornly unyielding, obstinate), *dogma* (a system of principles or beliefs, a prescribed doctrine)

dys: faulty, abnormal
dysfunctional (impaired or abnormal in function), *dyslexia* (an impaired ability to read)

eu: good, well

eulogy (a verbal or written tribute, especially one praising someone who has died), *euthanasia* (the act of painlessly ending the life of someone suffering from a terminal illness)

(h)etero: different, other

heterosexual (a person sexually attracted to members of the opposite sex), *heterodox* (disagreeing with or departing from accepted beliefs)

(h)omo: same

homogeneous (of the same or similar nature or kind; having a uniform structure or composition throughout), *homophone* (a word that sounds the same as another but has a different meaning)

hyper: over, excessive

hyperactive (highly or excessively active), *hyperventilate* (to breathe excessively and abnormally fast)

morph: shape

metamorphosis (a transformation, a marked change of form, character, or function), *polymorphous* (having or assuming a variety of forms)

SHORTCUT: USING MNEMONIC DEVICES

Mnemonic devices, as you know, are those tricks such as rhymes that we use to help us remember things. Use them to remember the meaning of word roots. For example, you can use the following catchy sentences to remember these roots:

My name is *Nom*.
He is hidden in the *crypt*.
Archie is a good ruler.
All the eggs are in the *pan*.
Phil loves to help others.

Here's a trick to remember the difference between *hetero* (different) and *homo* (same): *homo* has the same number of letters as *same*.

If you are a visual learner, again, use pictures to help you remember words. For example, to remember that the root *dog/dox* means opinion, you can imagine a dog explaining his opinion on an important issue. To remember that *eu* means good or well, you can picture the letters EU on a well.

nom, nym: name

nominate (to name as a candidate), *synonym* (a word having the same or nearly the same meaning as another)

pan: all, everyone

panorama (a complete view in every direction), *pantheon* (a temple dedicated to all the gods; all the gods of a people or region)

pas, pat, path: feeling, suffering, disease
compassion (deep awareness of and sympathy for another's suffering), *sympathy* (sharing another person's feelings; feeling pity or tenderness toward another's pain or suffering; harmony, agreement between two people)

ped: child, education
encyclopedia (a comprehensive reference work on a wide range of subjects), *pediatrician* (a physician specializing in the care of infants and children)

peri: around
perimeter (the outer limits or boundary of an area), *periscope* (an optical instrument that provides a view of an otherwise obstructed field)

phil: love
bibliophile (a lover of books), *philosophy* (love and pursuit of wisdom; a systematic investigation of questions about knowledge, existence, and ethics)

phone: sound
phonics (a method of teaching reading by training beginners to associate letters with their sound values), *symphony* (a long and complex sonata for an orchestra; a large orchestra)

theo: god
atheist (one who denies the existence of a god or supreme being), *theology* (the study of god and religion)

Now you have a larger store of word roots in your vocabulary—and a greater ability to break down unfamiliar words and use their roots to determine meaning. Keep reviewing common word roots as well as prefixes and suffixes as you prepare for your test. The more familiar you are with these word parts, the more accurately you will be able to determine the meaning of unfamiliar words and achieve a higher score on your exam.

CHEAT SHEET: ASSOCIATE AND ELIMINATE

Remember the power of two key vocabulary test strategies: association and elimination. Use association to remember root meanings and to determine the meaning of unfamiliar words. Use elimination to narrow down your answer choices on an exam. That way, even if you guess, you have a much better chance of guessing the correct answer.

TIPS AND STRATEGIES

Many words in the English language come from Greek word roots. Here again are some specific strategies for using your knowledge of word roots to build your vocabulary and improve your score on an exam.

- Take the time to memorize as many Greek word roots as you can. By memorizing these word bases, you will be able to learn new words more quickly and better determine the meaning of unfamiliar words.

- Use words that you are very familiar with as examples when you study word roots. The more familiar the word is to you (e.g., *incline*, *democracy*), the easier it will be for you to remember the meaning of the root word. Use words that create a vivid picture in your imagination.

- Remember that you use common word roots every day, often without realizing it. Do not feel intimidated by the long lists in this chapter or in Appendix A. It is likely that you already know a lot of this material.

- Remember that word roots work with prefixes and suffixes—and sometimes other root words—to create meaning. Look at all parts of the word and the context, if possible, to determine meaning.

- Remember the power of elimination on an exam. Use your knowledge of word roots to eliminate incorrect answers. The more you narrow down your choices, the better your chances of choosing the correct answer.

- Use the power of association. If you don't know or can't remember the root word, try to recall the meaning of another word that sounds like it or shares the same root word.

EXTRA HELP

If you would like additional review or further practice with word roots, see Lessons 7 and 8 in LearningExpress's *Vocabulary and Spelling Success in 20 Minutes a Day, 3rd edition*.

PRACTICE

Use your knowledge of word roots and prefixes and suffixes to choose the best answer to each question.

1. Something that is *unorthodox:*
   a. does not accurately represent reality.
   b. is mislabeled or misnamed.
   c. does not conform to traditionally held beliefs.
   d. is conspicuously out of place.
   e. is unable to function due to excessive wear and tear.

2. A *euphemism* is:
  a. a highly fatal disease.
  b. a nice word to replace something offensive.
  c. something rare, unique.
  d. a name with an ancient origin.
  e. a theory of education in which humanities should be emphasized over the sciences.

3. A *nominal* leader:
  a. does not have any real power.
  b. does not have any education.
  c. does not accurately represent his or her constituents.
  d. implements policies similar to his or her predecessor.
  e. believes him or herself to be a god.

4. Someone who is *apathetic:*
  a. is very sensitive to noise.
  b. is so dependent upon others he or she has difficulty functioning alone.
  c. lacks the strength to do what is right or good.
  d. shows a lack of concern or emotion.
  e. has difficulty determining his or her position on important issues.

5. A *panacea* is:
  a. a malfunctioning machine or appliance.
  b. a cure-all.
  c. a well-wisher.
  d. a secret lover.
  e. a copy or duplicate.

6. An *automaton* is:
  a. a musician.
  b. a world traveler.
  c. someone who frequently exaggerates.
  d. a robotic person.
  e. a disfigured person.

7. A person who is *peripatetic:*
  a. is poor, destitute.
  b. is in good health, both emotionally and physically.
  c. walks around from place to place.
  d. is related to royalty.
  e. is prone to excessive spending.

8. A *dystopia* is:

   a. an imaginary place filled with terror and oppression.

   b. a school devoted to religious training.

   c. an incision made by slicing diagonally through something.

   d. a congenital disease of the heart.

   e. an uneven or twisted path, especially one through a mountain.

9. A *heterogeneous* group:

   a. meets at the same time each week.

   b. is the group that determines the rules or regulations that others must abide by.

   c. is composed of very different people.

   d. donates money to numerous charities.

   e. is well-rounded and efficient.

10. A *hyperbole* is:

   a. a long detour.

   b. a great exaggeration.

   c. a similarity or sameness.

   d. a coincidence; something that happens at the same time.

   e. a token of support or encouragement.

11. Something that is *cryptic:*

   a. is known by name.

   b. is round or spherical in shape.

   c. is designed for very young children.

   d. has a secret meaning.

   e. shares the opinion of the majority.

12. A *diatribe* is:

   a. a bitter, cutting verbal attack.

   b. an unexpected test result.

   c. a self-destructive behavior.

   d. a large group of like-minded people.

   e. a heart-warming story, especially one in which family members are reunited.

13. Someone who is *pedantic:*

   a. enjoys playing music, especially with others.

   b. tends to favor one person over others although all have equal qualifications.

   c. refuses to listen to the opinions of others.

   d. is constantly trying to show how much he or she knows.

   e. is obsessed with a celebrity, especially one who is dead.

14. When there is *discord* between two people, there is:
   a. a deeply loving relationship.
   b. a lack of agreement or harmony.
   c. a shared opinion or belief.
   d. a mutual respect.
   e. an inability to respect the differences between them.

15. A *proclivity* is:
   a. an impairment; something that prevents something from working properly.
   b. a natural tendency or inclination.
   c. an unlikely friendship or cooperative effort between two or more people.
   d. a formal statement of one's beliefs.
   e. a regulation or rule that all must abide by.

16. Someone who is a *misanthrope:*
   a. loves meeting new people or having new experiences.
   b. changes his or her name frequently.
   c. tends to side with the majority or winning side.
   d. dutifully records events in a diary or journal.
   e. dislikes or distrusts most other people.

17. You have an *oligarchy* when:
   a. all sides are equal.
   b. the government is run by a few powerful people.
   c. there is widespread discontent among the members of an organization.
   d. there is a revolution in teaching methods or in a curriculum.
   e. there is an overabundance of material, supplies, etc.

18. A *pandemic* flu would:
   a. affect a great many people over a very large area.
   b. cause great suffering to an individual who contracts it.
   c. be annoying but essentially harmless.
   d. stem from an unknown or hidden source.
   e. last a long time and tend to recur frequently.

19. A *cacophony* is:
   a. something fake; a copy or forgery.
   b. an immature or childish person.
   c. a harsh or jarring sound; clamor.
   d. a tribute to a deity.
   e. something tangled or twisted; a complex or intricate design or shape.

20. An *apotheosis* is:
   a. a medical doctor specializing in hereditary diseases.
   b. a belief in the supremacy of human beings.
   c. a refusal to acknowledge similarities between two people, ideas, etc.
   d. a glorification, the elevation of a person to a divine status.
   e. a means of removing obstructions without causing damage to the existing structure.

21. *Anthropomorphic* means:
   a. attributing human characteristics to an animal or object.
   b. functioning independently.
   c. reduced to the smallest possible amount; the core.
   d. named after an ancestor.
   e. something that is required in order for something else to take place; a prerequisite.

22. A *paradox* is something that:
   a. is highly offensive.
   b. has a three-dimensional shape or form.
   c. seems to contradict a generally accepted opinion.
   d. a trick or sleight of hand; something cunning or deceitful.
   e. has a beneficial effect, especially on health.

23. *Demography* is the study of:
   a. disease.
   b. abnormal behaviors.
   c. types or systems of government.
   d. human populations.
   e. religious figures, especially saints.

24. If you feel a *disinclination* towards something, you feel:
   a. passion.
   b. reluctance.
   c. a strong connection, synergy.
   d. pity.
   e. discomfort.

25. A *dichotomy* is:
    a. a cutting or dividing into two parts.
    b. something used to diagnose personality disorders.
    c. a chamber in the heart.
    d. a tool used to bend something that is straight.
    e. a universal principle or belief.

ANSWERS

1. c. The prefix *un-* means not, against. The root *dog/dox* means opinion. *Unorthodox* means breaking with convention or tradition, not orthodox; nonconformist.

2. b. The root *eu* means good, well. The noun suffix *-ism* means state or doctrine of. A *euphemism* is a mild or inoffensive word or phrase substituted for one that is considered harsh or offensive.

3. a. The root *nom/nym* means name; the adjective suffix *-al* means of or relating to. *Nominal* means of or relating to names; existing in name only, not real; so small as to be trivial or insignificant. Thus, a nominal leader is a leader in name only and has no real power.

4. d. The prefix *a-* means not, without. The root *pas/pat/path* means feeling, suffering, disease. The adjective suffix *-ic* means pertaining or relating to, having the quality of. *Apathetic* means feeling or showing a lack of interest, concern, or emotion; indifferent, unresponsive.

5. b. The root *pan* means all, everyone. A *panacea* is a remedy of all ills, evils, difficulties, or diseases; a cure-all.

6. d. The root *auto* means self. An *automaton* is someone who acts or responds in a mechanical or robotic way; a self-operating or automatic machine, a robot.

7. c. The root *peri* means around. The adjective suffix *-ic* means pertaining or relating to, having the quality of. *Peripatetic* means walking about from place to place, itinerant.

8. a. The root *dys* means faulty, abnormal. The noun suffix *-ia* identifies names or diseases. A *dystopia* is an imaginary state in which the condition of life is extremely bad, as from deprivation, terror, or oppression; a story describing such a state.

9. c. The Greek root *hetero* means different, other; the Latin root *gen* means birth, kind. The adjective suffix *-ous* means having the quality of or relating to. *Heterogeneous* means consisting of elements or parts that are dissimilar, unrelated, not of the same kind or nature.

10. b. The root *hyper* means over, excessive. A *hyperbole* is a figure of speech using exaggeration for emphasis or effect.

11. d. The root *cryp* means hidden. The adjective suffix *-ic* means pertaining or relating to, having the quality of. *Cryptic* means having a hidden or secret meaning, mysterious; hidden, secret, occult.

12. a. The root *dia* means apart, through. A *diatribe* means a bitter, abusive verbal attack; an acrimonious denunciation.

13. d. The root *ped* means child, education. The adjective suffix *-ic* means pertaining or relating to, having the quality of. *Pedantic* means marked by a narrow, tiresome focus on or display of learning, especially of rules or trivial matters.

14. b. The prefix *dis-* means away from, apart, reversal, not. The root *card/cord/cour* means heart. *Discord* means a lack of agreement or harmony among persons, groups, or things; tension resulting from such disagreement.

15. b. The prefix *pro-* means for, forward. The root *cli/clin* means to lean toward, bend. The noun suffix *-ity* means state of being. *Proclivity* means a natural tendency, disposition, or inclination; predisposition.

16. e. The prefix *mis-* means wrong, ill. The root *anthro/andro* means man, human. A *misanthrope* is one who hates or distrusts mankind.

17. b. The root *arch/archi/archy* means chief, principal, ruler. An *oligarchy* is a form of government in which the power is in the hands of a few people. *Olig* means few.

18. a. The root *pan* means all, everyone; the root *de* means people. The adjective suffix *-ic* means pertaining or relating to, having the quality of. A *pandemic* is an epidemic affecting a wide geographical area and affecting a large portion of the population.

19. c. The root *phone* means sound. A *cacophony* is a loud, jarring, discordant sound; clamor, din.

20. d. The root *theo* means god. The noun suffix *-sis* means the process of. An *apotheosis* is a deification, an exalted or glorified ideal.

21. a. The root *anthro/andro* means man, human; the root *morph* means shape. The adjective suffix *-ic* means pertaining or relating to, having the quality of. *Anthropomorphic* means attributing human characteristics, motivations, or behavior to animals or inanimate objects.

22. c. The prefix *para-* means beside. The root *dog/dox* means opinion. A *paradox* is a statement that seems to be contradictory or absurd but may nonetheless be true, a self-contradictory assertion; a statement contrary to received opinion.

23. d. The root *dem* means people. The noun suffix *-graphy* means writing about or representation of a specific subject or object. *Demography* means the study of the characteristics of human populations, such as size, growth, births, mortality, and economic standing.

24. b. The prefix *dis-* means away from, apart, reversal, not. The root *cli/clin* means to lean toward, bend. The noun suffix *-tion* means action, process, or the result of an action or process; state, condition, or quality of. *Disinclination* means a mild dislike, unwillingness, reluctance; a lack of inclination.

25. a. The root *di/dia* means apart, through. The noun suffix *-y* means condition, state, or quality. A *dichotomy* is a division into two usually contradictory parts or kinds.

WORD LIST

amorphous (ă·ˈmor·fŭs) *adj.* 1. having no definite form or distinct shape; shapeless 2. of no particular kind or character, anomalous.

anachronism (ă·ˈnak·rŏ·niz·ĕm) *n.* 1. something that is placed into an incorrect historical period 2. a person, custom, or idea that is out of date.

anarchy (ˈan·ăr·kee) *n.* 1. the complete absence of government or control resulting in lawlessness 2. political disorder and confusion.

anthropomorphic (an·thrŏ·pŏ·ˈmor·fik) *adj.* attributing human characteristics, motivations, or behavior to animals or inanimate objects.

apathetic (ap·ă·ˈthet·ik) *adj.* feeling or showing a lack of interest, concern, or emotion; indifferent, unresponsive.

apotheosis (ă·poth·i·ˈoh·sis) *n.* deification, an exalted or glorified ideal.

automaton (aw·ˈtom·ă·tŏn) *n.* someone who acts or responds in a mechanical or robotic way 2. a self·operating or automatic machine, a robot.

autonomy (aw·ˈton·ŏ·mee) *n.* personal or political independence; self·government, self·determination.

cacophony (kă·ˈkof·ŏ·nee) *n.* loud, jarring, discordant sound; clamor, din.

chronic (ˈkron·ik) *adj.* 1. continuing for a long time; on·going, habitual 2. long·lasting or recurrent.

chronicle (ˈkron·i·kĕl) *n.* a detailed record or narrative description of past events; *v.* to record in chronological order; make a historical record.

chronological (kron·ŏ·ˈloj·i·kăl) *adj.* relating to chronology; arranged in order of time of occurrence.

chronology (krŏ·ˈnol·ŏ·jee) *n.* the arrangement of events in time; the sequence in which events occurred.

chronometer (krŏ·ˈnom·i·tĕr) *n.* an exceptionally accurate clock; a precise instrument for measuring time.

cryptic (ˈkrip·tik) *adj.* having a hidden or secret meaning, mysterious; hidden, secret, occult.

demography (di·ˈmog·ră·fee) *n.* the study of the characteristics of human populations, such as size, growth, births, mortality, and economic standing.

diatribe (ˈdī·ă·trīb) *n.* a bitter, abusive verbal attack; an acrimonious denunciation.

dichotomy (dī·ˈkot·ŏ·mee) *n.* division into two usually contradictory parts or kinds.

discord (ˈdis·kord) *n.* 1. a lack of agreement or harmony among persons, groups, or things; tension resulting from such disagreement 2. a harsh or jarring sound or combination of sounds.

disinclination (dis·in·kli·'nay·shŏn) *n.* a mild dislike, unwillingness, or reluctance; a lack of inclination.

dogmatic (dawg·'mat·ik) *adj.* 1. asserting something in a positive, absolute, arrogant way 2. of or relating to dogma.

dystopia (dis·'to·pi·ă) *n.* 1. an imaginary state in which the condition of life is extremely bad, as from deprivation, terror, or oppression 2. a story describing such a state.

empathy ('em·pă·thee) *n.* understanding and identifying with another's feelings, situation, or motives.

euphemism ('yoo·fĕ·miz·ĕm) *n.* a mild or inoffensive word or phrase substituted for one that is considered harsh or offensive, e.g., *passed away.*

euphoria (yoo·'fohr·i·ă) *n.* a feeling of well·being or high spirits.

heterogeneous (het·ĕ·rŏ·'jee·ni·ŭs) *adj.* consisting of elements or parts that are dissimilar, unrelated, not of the same kind or nature.

homogeneous (hoh·mŏ·'jee·ni·ŭs) *adj.* of the same or similar nature or kind; having a uniform structure or composition throughout.

hyperbole (hī·'pur·bŏ·lee) *n.* a figure of speech using exaggeration for emphasis or effect, e.g., *I've told you a million times.*

misanthrope (mis·'an·throhp) *n.* one who hates or distrusts humankind.

nominal ('nom·ĭ·năl) *adj.* 1. of or relating to a name or names 2. existing in name only, not real 3. so small as to be trivial or insignificant.

oligarchy ('ol·ĭ·gahr·kee) *n.* a form of government in which the power is in the hands of a few people.

panacea (pan·ă·'see·ă) *n.* a remedy for all ills, evils, difficulties, or diseases; a cure·all.

pandemic (pan·'dem·ik) *adj.* 1. widespread, existing everywhere; *n.* an epidemic affecting a wide geographical area and affecting a large portion of the population.

pandemonium (pan·dĕ·'moh·ni·ŭm) *n.* a state of extreme disorder or chaos; a wild uproar, noisy confusion.

paradox ('par·ă·doks) *n.* 1. a statement that seems to be contradictory or absurd but may nonetheless be true; a self·contradictory assertion 2. a statement contrary to received opinion.

pedantic (pi·'dăn·tik) *adj.* marked by a narrow, tiresome focus on or display of learning, especially of rules or trivial matters.

peripatetic (per·i·pă·'tet·ik) *adj.* walking about from place to place; itinerant.

peripheral (pĕ·'rif·ĕ·răl) *adj.* 1. of or relating to the periphery or edge; on the outer boundary 2. not of central importance or relevance.

philanthropy (fi·'lan·thrŏ·pee) *n.* 1. love of humankind 2. voluntary action intended to promote the welfare of others; an institution dedicated to this.

proclivity (proh·'kliv·i·tee) *n.* a natural tendency, disposition, or inclination; predisposition.

pseudonym ('soo·dŏ·nim) *n.* a fictitious name, especially a pen name used by a writer.

synchronize ('sing·krŏ·nīz) *v.* 1. to cause to occur at the same time 2. to cause to agree in time 3. to occur at the same time, be simultaneous.

unorthodox (un·'or·thŏ·doks) *adj.* breaking with convention or tradition, not orthodox; nonconformist.

6

Homophones and Other Commonly Confused Words

Do you know when to use *accept* instead of *except*? *Ensure* instead of *assure*? *Incredulous* instead of *incredible*? Using the right word can make the difference between confusion and clarity—and have a huge impact on your exam score. This chapter briefly reviews some of the most common homophones and then focuses on commonly confused words that you are likely to encounter on your exam. Before you begin your study of commonly confused words, take a few minutes to take this ten-question *Benchmark Quiz*. These questions are similar to the type of questions that you will find on important tests. When you are finished, check the answer key carefully to assess your results. Your Benchmark Quiz analysis will help you determine how much time you need to spend on this area as well as the specific words you need to learn in order to increase your vocabulary power. A complete list of the vocabulary words used in this lesson is provided at the end of the chapter.

BENCHMARK QUIZ

Choose the correct word in the parenthesis to complete each sentence.

1. Lilin (*alluded/eluded*) to problems with her boss, but she didn't say anything directly.

2. Xiu is coming this afternoon to determine the (*extant/extent*) of the problem.

3. The checks were (*disbursed/dispersed*) this morning.

4. Once again, Luna has come up with an (*ingenious/ingenuous*) solution to the problem.

5. We will (*waive/wave*) the late fee because of your extenuating circumstances.

6. Please (*precede/proceed*) with caution through the construction zone.

7. Reina is in (*eminent/imminent/emanate*) danger and needs our help right away.

8. Jillian met with a lawyer to see if her landlord could be (*persecuted/prosecuted*) for his negligence regarding her apartment building.

9. It was a grueling six-hour (*ascent/assent*) from our camp to the top of the mountain.

10. Here is a list of the books the school librarian would like to (*censor/censure/sensor*) because she feels they are inappropriate for children.

BENCHMARK QUIZ SOLUTIONS

How did you do on identifying the correct word? Check your answers here, and then analyze the results to figure out your plan of attack for mastering this topic.

▶ Answers

1. **alluded.** To *allude* means to make an indirect reference to.

2. **extent.** *Extent* means the range, distance, or degree to which something reaches or extends.

3. disbursed. To *disburse* means to pay out.

4. ingenious. *Ingenious* means marked by inventive skill or creativity; showing inventiveness and skill, remarkably clever.

5. waive. To *waive* is to give up (a right or claim) voluntarily, relinquish; to refrain from enforcing or insisting upon (a rule, penalty, standard procedure, etc.).

6. proceed. To *proceed* means to go forward or onward, especially after an interruption; move on, advance.

7. imminent. *Imminent* means about to occur, impending.

8. prosecuted. To *prosecute* is to bring a criminal action against (someone).

9. ascent. An *ascent* is an upward slope; a movement upward, advancement.

10. censor. To *censor* is to forbid the publication, distribution, or other public dissemination of something because it is considered obscene or otherwise politically or morally unacceptable.

BENCHMARK QUIZ RESULTS

If you answered 8–10 questions correctly, well done! You are already familiar with some of the most common homophones and frequently confused words. Give the lesson a quick review and do the practice exercise. If your score on the practice test is equally high, move on to Chapter 7.

If you answered 4–7 questions correctly, you seem to be familiar with some of the most common homophones and frequently confused words. But you need more practice to really sharpen this skill. Be sure to set aside some time to carefully review the commonly confused word sets listed in this chapter.

If you answered 1–3 questions correctly, you need to learn how to differentiate between homophones and other commonly confused words in order to build an effective vocabulary and communicate clearly. Study the lesson that follows carefully, and do the practice quiz on a separate sheet of paper so that you can do the exercise several times if necessary. Take extra time to learn the commonly confused word groups in this chapter and use the source listed in **Extra Help** at the end of the chapter for more review and practice.

JUST IN TIME LESSON—
COMMONLY CONFUSED WORDS

Imagine that you are reading a story to a child and you come across the following sentence:

> *The night sleighed the dragon.*

Chances are the child would have no trouble understanding what you read, but because you see the words on paper, you can see that something is wrong: the writer has confused two different homophones. As a result, the written sentence means something very different from what the writer intended and what the child understands. Indeed, the written version is not only incorrect; it is also illogical.

A homophone is exactly what its two Greek roots suggest:

homo	*phone*
same	sound

It is a word that sounds the same as another but has a different meaning. *Night* and *knight*, for example, are homophones, as are *slay* and *sleigh*, *great* and *grate*, and *bear/bare*. There are dozens of homophones, many of which you already know by heart, others that you may still find confusing. If so, this chapter will help you get them straight.

◼◼◼◼◼◼ GLOSSARY

HOMOPHONE a word that sounds the same as another but has a different meaning and spelling

Spelling and grammar tests will often ask you to determine the correct homophone for a given context—whether you should use *whether* or *weather* in a sentence, for example, or *piece* or *peace*. It is very important to know your homophones and use them correctly. Otherwise, you may confuse your readers with sentences that are at best incorrect and at worst unintelligible. So take some time to review the homophones in the listing on the following page. Then go on to the rest of the lesson. Although homophones like *farther* and *further* may be confusing, they aren't likely to appear on the vocabulary section of a test like the Postal Worker exam, the PSAT exam, or even the GRE General test. The rest of this lesson will review the kind of commonly confused words you are more likely to encounter on your exam.

COMMON HOMOPHONES AND OTHER FREQUENTLY CONFUSED WORDS

The following listing shows some of the most common homophones and other frequently confused word pairs along with a brief definition of each word.

Confusing Words	Quick Definition
accept	recognize
except	excluding
access	means of approaching
excess	extra
adapt	to adjust
adopt	to take as one's own
affect	to influence
effect (noun)	result
effect (verb)	to bring about
all ready	totally prepared
already	by this time
all ways	every method
always	forever
among	in the middle of several
between	in an interval separating (two)
assure	to make certain (assure someone)
ensure	to make certain
insure	to make certain (financial value)
beside	next to
besides	in addition to
bibliography	list of writings
biography	a life story
breath(noun)	respiration
breathe (verb)	to inhale and exhale
breadth	width

Confusing Words	Quick Definition
capital (noun)	money
capital (adjective)	most important
capitol	government building
complement	match
compliment	praise
disinterested	no strong opinion either way
uninterested	unengaged; having no interest in
envelop	surround
envelope	paper wrapping for a letter
farther	beyond
further	additional
immigrate	enter a new country
emigrate	leave a country
imply	hint, suggest
infer	assume, deduce
loose	not tight
lose	unable to find
may be	something may possibly be
maybe	perhaps
overdo	do too much
overdue	late
personal	individual
personnel	employees
precede	go before
proceed	continue
proceeds	profits
principal (adjective)	main
principal (noun)	person in charge
principle	standard

Confusing Words	Quick Definition
stationary	still, not moving
stationery	writing material
than	in contrast to
then	next in time
their	belonging to them
there	in a place
they're	they are
weather	climate
whether	if
who	substitute for he, she or they
whom	substitute for him, her or them
your	belonging to you
you're	you are

COMMONLY CONFUSED WORDS—THE NEXT LEVEL

Now it's time for the more sophisticated sets of commonly confused words—groups of two or three words in which at least one is a good candidate for a vocabulary exam. For example, here's a pair of words you should already be familiar with: *team/teem*. Remember *teem* from Chapter 2? This is a commonly tested vocabulary word and a homophone. Chances are you won't confuse *teem* with *team*, since *team* is such a familiar word. But you should know what *teem* means and make it part of your vocabulary as you prepare for your exam.

Another important reason to review homophones like *team/teem* and *waive/wave* is to avoid a trap sometimes set by the test developers. That is, you might encounter questions that use the definition of a familiar homophone as a distracter. Here is an example:

> To *waive* means:
> **a.** to signal with an up and down or back and forth movement.
> **b.** to return to the original starting point.
> **c.** to relinquish a right or claim.
> **d.** to swell up or rise to the surface.
> **e.** to violate a rule or law.

The correct answer is **c**. *Waive* means to give up (a right or claim) voluntarily, relinquish; to refrain from enforcing or insisting upon (a rule, penalty, standard procedure, etc.). If you don't know the meaning of *waive*, however, you might be tempted to choose **a**, which is the definition of its homophone *wave*, or **d**, which is related to the definition of a wave. These answer choices are tempting because they sound familiar. You need to be able to recognize the familiar homophone and recall its definition.

Not all commonly confused words are homophones. Take *disinterested* and *uninterested* as an example. They don't sound the same because they have very distinct prefixes. But the prefixes are attached to the same root, and the prefixes seem to have essentially the same meaning: *dis* means away from, apart, reversal, not; *un* means not, against. Thus many people assume that both words mean the same thing: *not* interested. However, only *uninterested* has this meaning. *Disinterested* means impartial or unbiased, free of selfish motives or interests—a different word entirely.

Some commonly confused words are particularly puzzling because the words not only sound similar, but they also have similar meanings. Take the homophones *cue* and *queue*, for example. Both mean a line of waiting people or vehicles, although *queue* is used far more often than *cue* for this meaning. Only *cue* also means a signal, such as a word or action, given to prompt or remind someone of something—and this is its most common usage. *Queue* means an ordered list of tasks to be performed or sequence of programs awaiting processing on a computer.

You already know many homophones and commonly confused words inside and out. The ones you don't know, you simply need to memorize. The question is, how do you remember these differences in meaning, especially when the words seem so much alike? The key is to capitalize on the differences in the words, and when it comes to frequently confused words, mnemonic devices come in especially handy. Take the commonly confused pair *ingenious* and *ingenuous*, for example:

> *ingenious:* marked by inventive skill or creativity; showing inventiveness and skill, remarkably clever.
> *ingenuous:* 1. not cunning or deceitful, unable to mask feelings; artless, frank, sincere 2. lacking sophistication or worldliness.

The only difference in the spelling of these words is the *i/u*. You can use this difference to remember key words in the definition of each word:

> *ingen<u>i</u>ous:* <u>i</u>nventive
> *ingen<u>u</u>ous:* <u>u</u>nable to mask feelings

Similarly, the difference between *disinterested* and *uninterested* is the prefix. Use this to help you remember the meaning: a *dis*interested person is *dis*tanced from the situation and is therefore impartial.

Here is a list of 25 commonly confused word sets that include important vocabulary words for your exam. The list includes the vocabulary words from the Benchmark Quiz and lesson.

WORD LIST

allude (ă·ˈlood) *v.* to make an indirect reference to.

elude (i·ˈlood) *v.* 1. to escape from or evade, especially by cleverness, daring, or skill 2. to be incomprehensible to, escape the understanding of.

appraise (ă·ˈprayz) *v.* 1. to evaluate 2. to establish value or estimate the worth of.

apprise (ă·ˈprīz) *v.* to give notice or information to; to make aware of, inform.

ascent (ă·ˈsent) *n.* 1. an upward slope 2. a movement upward, advancement.

assent (ă·ˈsent) *n.* agreement; concurrence; consent.

censor (ˈsen·sŏr) *v.* to forbid the publication, distribution, or other public dissemination of something because it is considered obscene or otherwise politically or morally unacceptable; *n.* an official who reviews books, films, etc. to remove what is considered morally, politically, or otherwise objectionable.

censure (ˈsen·shŭr) *n.* expression of strong criticism or disapproval; a rebuke or condemnation; *v.* to criticize strongly, rebuke, condemn.

sensor (ˈsen·sŏr) *n.* a device that receives and responds to a stimulus such as light, smoke, etc.

cue (kyoo) *n.* 1. a signal, such as a word or action, given to prompt or remind someone of something; a hint or suggestion 2. a line of waiting people or vehicles; a queue.

queue (kyoo) *n.* 1. a line of waiting people or vehicles 2. (in information processing) an ordered list of tasks to be performed or sequence of programs awaiting processing.

decent (ˈdee·sĕnt) *adj.* 1. conforming to what is socially or morally suitable or correct 2. meeting acceptable standards; sufficient, adequate.

descent (di·ˈsent) *n.* 1. the act of descending or moving downward; a downward slope or movement 2. hereditary derivation; lineage.

dissent (di·ˈsent) *v.* 1. to differ in opinion, disagree 2. to withhold approval or assent; *n.* 1. a difference of opinion 2. nonconformity.

deprecate ('dep·rĕ·kayt) *v.* to express disapproval of; to belittle, depreciate.

depreciate (di·'pree·shi·ayt) *v.* 1. to diminish in price or value; to lessen the worth of 2. to think or speak of as being of little worth; to belittle.

disburse (dis·'burs) *v.* to pay out.

disperse (di·'spurs) *v.* 1. to separate and scatter in different directions; to cause to do so 2. to distribute widely, disseminate.

disinterested (dis·'in·tĕ·res·tid) *adj.* impartial or unbiased, free of selfish motives or interests.

uninterested (un·'in·tĕ·ris·tid) *adj.* not interested; having no care or interest in knowing.

elicit (i·'lis·it) *v.* 1. to call forth or draw out; to provoke 2. to deduce or derive by reasoning.

illicit (i·'lis·it) *adj.* illegal, forbidden by law; contrary to accepted morality or convention.

eminent ('em·ĭ·nĕnt) *adj.* towering above or more prominent than others, lofty; standing above others in quality, character, reputation, etc.; distinguished.

imminent ('im·ĭ·nĕnt) *adj.* about to occur; impending.

emanate ('em·ă·nayt) *v.* to come or issue forth, as from a source.

extant ('ek·stănt) *adj.* still in existence; not extinct, destroyed or lost.

extent (ik·'stent) *n.* 1. the range, distance, or degree to which something reaches or extends 2. a wide and open space or area.

SHORTCUT:
A STITCH IN TIME SAVES NINE

You may think that you don't have the time to come up with rhymes or other mnemonic devices to remember the meanings of these commonly confused words—you have too much studying to do. But spending the time now to create something you can easily remember can save you a great deal of time later on by drastically reducing your review time. Plus, it will also help you build a stronger and more accurate vocabulary because you will be able to accurately remember the meaning of a word.

fain (fayn) *adv.* with joy; gladly.

feign (fayn) *v.* to pretend, to give the false appearance of.

faux (foh) *adj.* artificial, fake; not genuine or real.

foe (foh) *n.* an enemy, adversary, or opponent.

hoard (hohrd) *n.* a hidden store or stock, cache; *v.* to collect and lay up; to amass and store in secret.

horde (hohrd) *n.* a large group or crowd; a vast multitude.

incredible (in·′kred·ĭ·bĕl) *adj.* 1. implausible, beyond belief 2. astonishing.

incredulous (in·′krej·ŭ·lŭs) *adj.* skeptical, unwilling to believe.

ingenious (in·′jeen·yŭs) *adj.* marked by inventive skill or creativity; showing inventiveness and skill, remarkably clever.

ingenuous (in·′jen·yoo·ŭs) *adj.* 1. not cunning or deceitful, unable to mask feelings; artless, frank, sincere 2. lacking sophistication or worldliness.

meddle (′med·ĕl) *v.* to intrude in other people's affairs; interfere.

mettle (′met·ĕl) *n.* courage, fortitude, spirit.

peak (peek) *v.* to reach its highest point or maximum development, activity, or intensity *n.* 1. the sharp end of something tapering to a point 2. the pointed top of a mountain, summit 3. the highest possible point of development, activity, or intensity.

peek (peek) *v.* to glance quickly or peer at furtively; *n.* a brief or furtive look.

pique (peek) *v.* 1. to cause annoyance or irritation; to vex or create resentment 2. to provoke or arouse.

persecute (′pur·sĕ·kyoot) *v.* to oppress, harass, or mistreat, especially because of race, religious or political beliefs, or sexual orientation.

prosecute (′pros·ĕ·kyoot) *v.* 1. to bring a criminal action against 2. to carry on, continue, practice.

precede (pri·′seed) *v.* to come or go before in time, place, rank, or importance.

proceed (prŏ·′seed) *v.* to go forward or onward, especially after an interruption; move on, advance.

prescribe (pri·ˈskrīb) *v.* 1. to issue commands, order something to be done; dictate 2. to order a medicine or other treatment.

proscribe (proh·ˈskrīb) *v.* to prohibit, forbid by law.

raise (rayz) *v.* 1. to lift, make higher; put in an upright position 2. to increase in size, quantity, intensity, degree, or strength; *n.* 1. the act of raising or increasing 2. an increase in salary.

raze (rayz) *v.* 1. to level to the ground, demolish completely 2. to erase, obliterate.

team (teem) *v.* to join together so as to form a team; *n.* a group organized to work together; a cooperative unit.

teem (teem) *v.* to be full of; to be present in large numbers.

waive (wayv) *v.* 1. to give up (a right or claim) voluntarily, relinquish 2. to refrain from enforcing or insisting upon (a rule, penalty, standard procedure, etc.); dispense with.

wave (wayv) *v.* 1. to move up and down or back and forth; undulate 2. to signal with an up and down or back and forth movement of the hand; *n.* 1. a ridge or swell on the surface of a body of water 2. a back-and-forth or up-and-down movement, especially of the hand 3. a surge, rush, or sudden great rise.

EXTRA HELP

Need more practice with homophones and other commonly confused words? Try Chapter 11 on homophones in LearningExpress's *1001 Vocabulary and Spelling Questions, 2nd edition*—it gives you 40 practice questions on the most common homophones.

TIPS AND STRATEGIES

Homophones and other frequently confused words can be particularly challenging, especially when you have a limited amount of time to prepare for an exam. Here are some specific tips and strategies to help you make the most of your study time:

- Spelling is often the key to distinguishing between commonly confused words. *Meddle*, for example, differs from *mettle* only by a *d* instead of a *t*. Use this key difference to help you remember the difference in meaning as well. For example, you might remember that *meddle* with a *d* is something you <u>d</u>on't want to do unless you want to annoy others.

- Review, review, review. Use flashcards or other study strategies to review these commonly confused words until you have them memorized, and then review them again.
- *Use* these words. If you use these words in your everyday writing and conversations, you will remember which word has which meaning. Or teach them to someone else. Teaching something to another person is one of the most effective ways to master that material.
- Remember to make the most of your learning style. Use whatever study or memorization techniques work best for you. For example, if you are a visual learner, create pictures that will help you remember word meanings. If you are an auditory learner, rhymes will be more effective.
- Pay attention to details, and use them to help you remember the words and their meanings. The more carefully you read each definition and the closer you look at the spelling of each word, the more likely you are to find a key for you to remember the differences between them. For example, *appraise* has the word *praise* in it. You can associate praise with a good evaluation, and *appraise* means to evaluate.
- Use your ears for the commonly confused words that aren't homophones, and use the difference in pronunciation to help you further differentiate between the words.
- Don't forget to use word parts to remember meaning. Both *prescribe* and *proscribe*, for example, have the root *scrib/script*, meaning to write. Then you can remember that *proscribe* is a (written) law that *pro*hibits something.

PRACTICE

Choose the correct word in the parenthesis to complete the sentence.

1. The pond was (*teaming/teeming*) with tadpoles after the frog eggs hatched.

2. Anita's (*faux/foe*) mink coat looked so real that a group of teenagers accused her of cruelty to animals.

3. Jackson may act as if he is totally (*disinterested/uninterested*) in you, but believe me, he is very anxious to learn more about you.

4. I am having the jewelry I inherited from my grandmother (*appraised/apprised*) to find out how much it is worth.

5. Helen entered the room right on (*cue/queue*).

6. You are sure to be (*censored/censured/sensored*) if you make such wild accusations about your colleagues.

7. The boy would (*fain/feign*) sleep rather than attend another evening piano recital given by his sister.

8. I have always admired Don's (*meddle/mettle*); he seems to be afraid of no one and nothing.

9. A (*hoard/horde*) of angry parents attended the school board meeting and demanded that the superintendent step down.

10. The documentary really (*peaked/peeked/piqued*) my interest in the Civil War.

11. With just a few hours to go before the big ceremony, Adele rushed around (*prescribing/proscribing*) orders left and right.

12. Huang decided to (*raise/raze*) the stakes by increasing the reward.

13. Although Oscar's story sounds (*incredible/incredulous*), I think he's telling the truth.

14. Jing-Mae gave her (*ascent/assent*) to the proposal, even though she did not entirely agree with the plan.

15. This looks like a (*decent/descent/dissent*) restaurant; let's eat here.

16. I tried everything, but nothing would (*elicit/illicit*) a response from the child.

17. The Euro has (*deprecated/depreciated*), but the dollar is up.

18. Stop (*persecuting/prosecuting*) me just because I often disagree with you.

19. Tomorrow the city is going to (*raise/raze*) the building that I grew up in.

20. As soon as I get off the phone, I will (*appraise/apprise*) you of the situation.

21. The odor quickly (*disbursed/dispersed*) through the room, and soon it was no longer even noticeable.

22. We have enough to do dealing with (*extant/extent*) problems regarding the excavation; don't worry me with things that *might* go wrong in the future.

23. I don't like Igor because he is constantly (*meddling/mettling*) in things that are none of his business.

24. Although you all seem to agree, I must (*decent/descent/dissent*); I think this is a bad decision.

25. Dixie is so (*ingenious/ingenuous*) I don't think she could lie if her life depended on it.

26. I'm just going to (*peak/peek/pique*) in the baby's room to make sure she's okay.

27. The thief managed to (*allude/elude*) the police for several days, but they finally caught up with him in Reno.

28. The (*cue/queue*) for the movies was all the way to the end of the block and around the corner.

29. Georgio had to (*fain/feign*) excitement when he opened his presents so his parents wouldn't know he'd already searched their room to find out what he was getting.

30. Jillian thought her landlord should be (*persecuted/prosecuted*) for his refusal to maintain her building.

31. A strange odor is (*eminenting/imminenting/emanating*) from Professor VanBuren's laboratory.

32. A good manager is always careful not to (*deprecate/depreciate*) an employee in front of others.

33. In the final scene, the hero defeats his life-long (*faux/foe*) in a deadly battle.

34. When we cleaned out the attic, we discovered that Grandma had a (*hoard/horde*) of extra cash hidden in an old trunk.

35. He is the most (*eminent/imminent/emanate*) judge in this state; everybody respects him.

36. We need a (*disinterested/uninterested*) third party to mediate this conflict.

37. When the children began neglecting their homework and chores, Rajita decided to (*prescribe/proscribe*) television viewing except on weekends.

38. Inessa couldn't believe Hitta was guilty and remained (*incredible/incredulous*) even after hearing all of the evidence.

39. I think Chapter 12 should (*precede/proceed*) Chapter 11, because Chapter 12 lays the foundation for what is discussed in Chapter 11.

40. What seemed like an (*elicit/illicit*) relationship between Lotta and one of her employees turned out to be a harmless friendship.

ANSWERS

1. teeming. To *teem* means to be full of, to be present in large numbers.

2. faux. *Faux* means artificial, fake; not genuine or real.

3. uninterested. *Uninterested* means not interested, having no care or interest in knowing.

4. appraised. To *appraise* means to evaluate, to establish value or estimate the worth of.

5. cue. A *cue* is a signal, such as a word or action, given to prompt or remind someone of something; a hint or suggestion.

6. censured. To *censure* is to criticize strongly, rebuke, condemn.

7. fain. *Fain* means with joy, gladly.

8. mettle. *Mettle* means courage, fortitude, spirit.

9. horde. A *horde* is a large group or crowd, a vast multitude.

10. piqued. To *pique* is (1) to cause annoyance or irritation, to vex; (2) to provoke or arouse. This sentence uses the second meaning.

11. **prescribing.** To *prescribe* is to issue commands, order something to be done, dictate. It also means to order a medicine or other treatment.

12. **raise.** To *raise* is to lift, make higher; to increase in size, quantity, intensity, degree, or strength.

13. **incredible.** *Incredible* means implausible, beyond belief; astonishing.

14. **assent.** *Assent* means agreement, concurrence, consent.

15. **decent.** *Decent* means (1) conforming to what is socially or morally suitable or correct; (2) meeting acceptable standards, sufficient, adequate. This sentence uses the second meaning.

16. **elicit.** To *elicit* means (1) to call forth or draw out, to provoke; (2) to deduce or derive by reasoning. This sentence uses the first meaning.

17. **depreciated.** To *depreciate* means to diminish in price or value, to lessen the worth of. It also means to think or speak of as being of little worth, to belittle.

18. **persecuting.** To *persecute* is to oppress, harass, or mistreat, especially because of race, religious or political beliefs, or sexual orientation.

19. **raze.** To *raze* is (1) to level to the ground, demolish completely; (2) to erase, obliterate. This sentence uses the first meaning.

20. **apprise.** To *apprise* means to give notice or information to, to make aware of, inform.

21. **dispersed.** To *disperse* is (1) to separate and scatter in different directions, or cause to do so; (2) to distribute widely, disseminate. This sentence uses the first meaning.

22. **extant.** *Extant* means still in existence; not extinct, destroyed or lost.

23. **meddling.** To *meddle* is to intrude in other people's affairs, interfere.

24. **dissent.** To *dissent* is (1) to differ in opinion, disagree; (2) to withhold approval or assent. This sentence uses the first meaning.

25. **ingenuous.** *Ingenuous* means (1) not cunning or deceitful, unable to mask feelings; artless, frank sincere; (2) lacking sophistication or worldliness. This sentence uses the first meaning.

26. peek. To *peek* is to glance quickly or peer at furtively.

27. elude. To *elude* is (1) to escape from or evade, especially by cleverness, daring, or skill; (2) to be incomprehensible to, escape the understanding of.

28. queue. A *queue* is (1) a line of waiting people or vehicles; (2) in information processing, an ordered list of tasks to be performed or sequence of programs awaiting processing. This sentence uses the first meaning.

29. feign. To *feign* is to pretend, to give the false appearance of.

30. waive. To *waive* means to voluntarily give up your right to something.

31. emanating. To *emanate* is to come or issue forth, as from a source.

32. deprecate. To *deprecate* is to express disapproval of, to belittle, depreciate. *Depreciate* is also a correct answer, as it also means to think or speak of as being of little worth, to belittle. However, *deprecate* is more often used than *depreciate* in this context.

33. foe. A *foe* is an enemy, adversary, or opponent.

34. hoard. A *hoard* is a hidden store or stock, a cache.

35. eminent. *Eminent* means towering above or more prominent than others, lofty; standing above others in quality, character, reputation, etc.; distinguished.

36. disinterested. *Disinterested* means impartial or unbiased, free from selfish motives or interests.

37. proscribe. To *proscribe* means to prohibit, forbid by law.

38. incredulous. *Incredulous* means skeptical, unwilling to believe.

39. precede. To *precede* means to come or go before in time, place, rank, or importance.

40. illicit. *Illicit* means illegal, forbidden by law; contrary to accepted morality or convention.

7

Magnificent Modifiers

Countless times throughout the day, you call upon your pool of adjectives to describe the people, places, and things around you. Before you begin learning and reviewing modifiers, take a few minutes to take this ten-question *Benchmark Quiz*. These questions are similar to the type of questions that you will find on important tests. When you are finished, check the answer key carefully to assess your results. Your Benchmark Quiz analysis will help you determine how much time you need to spend on reviewing modifiers as well as the specific words you need to learn in order to increase your vocabulary power. This chapter presents 40 magnificent modifiers to help you build your vocabulary and improve your score on the exam.

BENCHMARK QUIZ

For questions 1–5, choose the best answer to complete each statement.

1. Something that is *hateful* is:
   a. paltry.
   b. latent.
   c. timid.
   d. odious.
   e. volatile.

2. Someone who is *intrepid* is:
   a. dangerous.
   b. detestable.
   c. fearless.
   d. a genius.
   e. extremely friendly.

3. Something that is *succinct* is:
   a. concise, to the point.
   b. sweet, succulent.
   c. distinct, standing out from others.
   d. easily copied or mimicked.
   e. indifferent, impassive.

4. Someone who is very *hesitant* and *shy* is best described as:
   a. stoic.
   b. steadfast.
   c. virulent.
   d. droll.
   e. timid.

5. Something that is *impervious* is:
   a. not able to be understood.
   b. not able to be penetrated.
   c. imperial, royal, suited for a king.
   d. easily influenced or swayed.
   e. transitory, lasting only a short time.

For questions 6–10, choose the word that best completes the sentence.

6. Your _____ support over the years has enabled me to achieve the success I enjoy today.
   a. pivotal
   b. resplendent
   c. steadfast
   d. furtive
   e. facetious

7. I don't trust Carl. He always acts in such a _____ manner that I believe he's hiding something.
   a. diffident
   b. egregious
   c. fervent
   d. furtive
   e. volatile

8. Raheeb was _____ enough to remain silent during Angelica's tirade.
   a. lax
   b. prudent
   c. scintillating
   d. strident
   e. surreptitious

9. Casey says he is completely through with LeeAnn, but she is convinced his love for her is simply in a/an _____ stage.
   a. dormant
   b. austere
   c. droll
   d. zealous
   e. pivotal

10. On his trip through the Amazon, Tyrell was bitten by a/an _____ insect and had to be hospitalized.
    a. adroit
    b. garrulous
    c. egregious
    d. paltry
    e. virulent

BENCHMARK QUIZ SOLUTIONS

How did you do on identifying magnificent modifiers? Check your answers here, and then analyze the results to figure out your plan of attack for mastering this topic.

▶ *Answers*

1. d. *Odious* means contemptible, hateful, detestable.

2. c. *Intrepid* means fearless, brave, undaunted.

3. a. *Succinct* means expressed clearly and precisely in few words; concise, terse.

4. e. *Timid* means lacking confidence, conviction, or courage; fearful, hesitant, shy.

5. b. *Impervious* means (1) incapable of being penetrated, (2) not able to be influenced or affected.

6. c. *Steadfast* means (1) firmly fixed or unchanging, resolute; (2) firmly loyal and constant, unswerving. This sentence uses the second meaning.

7. d. *Furtive* means (1) characterized by stealth or secrecy, surreptitious; (2) suggesting a hidden motive, shifty. This sentence uses the second meaning.

8. b. *Prudent* means careful and sensible regarding one's actions and interests; exercising good judgment, judicious.

9. a. *Dormant* means (1) lying asleep or as if asleep, inactive, at rest; (2) inactive but capable of becoming active; latent, temporarily quiescent. This sentence uses the second meaning.

10. e. *Virulent* means (1) extremely poisonous, injurious or infectious; (2) bitterly hostile or hateful, acrimonious. This sentence uses the first meaning.

BENCHMARK QUIZ RESULTS

If you answered 8–10 questions correctly, well done! You are already familiar with many of these magnificent modifiers. Give the lesson a quick review and do the practice exercise. If your score on the practice test is equally high, move on to Chapter 8.

If you answered 4–7 questions correctly, you know some of these useful adjectives, but you need more of these magnificent modifiers in your permanent vocabulary. Be sure to set aside some time to carefully review the adjectives listed in this chapter.

If you answered 1–3 questions correctly, it's time to expand the number of adjectives in your vocabulary and add some more sophisticated modifiers to your word base. Study the lesson that follows carefully, and do the practice quiz on a separate sheet of paper so that you can do the exercise several times if necessary. Also, see the sources listed in **Extra Help** for more review and practice.

JUST IN TIME LESSON—MAGNIFICENT MODIFIERS

While every sentence must contain a subject and verb, if you think about it, what most sentences do is *describe* people and places, objects and actions, feelings and ideas. Perhaps that's why you are likely to find more adjectives than any other part of speech on a vocabulary exam.

The English language is rich with adjectives to describe everything from personally traits to cooking techniques, from faraway places to intellectual achievements—all the people, places, and things around us. Well-chosen adjectives make your communications more effective and inviting by adding color, definition, and detail. They enable you to clarify and quantify ideas, paint vivid pictures for your readers and listeners, and elicit specific emotions as you express yourself to others. Consider, for example, how much the right adjectives enhance the following sentence:

He gave me a glance.
He gave me a quick glance.
He gave me a quick, furtive glance.

In the first sentence, you have no idea what sort of glance he gave. Was it a longing, wistful glance? A scornful glance? A sympathetic glance? We don't know; the possibilities are endless. In the second sentence, you get some information from the adjective *quick*, but not much, because it is the nature of a glance to be quick. The third sentence, however, gives you a real description by adding the word *furtive*, which means characterized by stealth or secrecy, surreptitious; suggesting a hidden motive, shifty. *Now* you can picture exactly what sort of glance he gave; everything hinges on this magnificent modifier.

An extensive vocabulary enables you to pull up the precise word to describe a person, place, thing, or situation and express the exact connotation you wish to convey. Notice how the right adjective pinpoints meaning and expresses ideas clearly and concisely in the following examples:

> *a question*
> *a clever question*
> *a <u>scintillating</u> question*

Scintillating means brilliantly clever and animated.

> *a mistake*
> *a really bad mistake*
> *an <u>egregious</u> mistake*

Egregious means conspicuously and outrageously bad or offensive; flagrant.

> *a fearless girl*
> *an undaunted girl*
> *an intrepid girl*

Here, the words *fearless, undaunted,* and *intrepid* all mean essentially the same thing, but each word has a different connotation and expresses a different degree of fearlessness. *Undaunted,* for example, suggests fearlessness combined with determination, while *intrepid* suggests fearlessness, determination, and strength, as well as risk-taking ability—it is the most powerful of these three words.

The 40 adjectives defined in this chapter appear regularly on vocabulary exams, but you will also come across them frequently in newspapers and textbooks, in your daily correspondence and conversations. Each definition includes a sample sentence to show you the word in context. Learn these adjectives well to improve your test score, to understand more of what you read, and to more accurately and colorfully describe the people, places, and things around you.

WORD LIST

adroit (ă·ˈdroit) *adj.* skillful, clever, or adept in action or in thought; dexterous, deft. *Priya is a very adroit seamstress; she should have your trousers fixed in no time.*

austere (aw·ˈsteer) *adj.* 1. severe or stern in attitude or appearance 2. simple, unadorned, very plain. *I know my dad seems austere, but he's really just a great big teddy bear.*

banal (bă·ˈnal) *adj.* commonplace, trite; obvious and uninteresting. *I was expecting something original and exciting, but the film turned out to have a banal storyline and mediocre acting.*

copious (ˈkoh·pi·ŭs) *adj.* large in number or quantity; abundant, plentiful. *The shipwrecked couple found a copious supply of coconut trees and shellfish on the island.*

diffident (ˈdif·i·dĕnt) *adj.* lacking self-confidence, shy and timid. *Alan used to be so diffident, but now he's as gregarious as can be and is usually the life of the party.*

SHORTCUT: FIND A SYNONYM

While it is important to know the full definition of a word to fully grasp its meaning, when you have a lot of words to learn and only a short time to learn them, focusing on synonyms can really help. After carefully reading each definition, choose a synonym that accurately conveys the meaning of the word, and memorize that synonym. For example, you can remember these words with their synonyms:

banal = trite
copious = plentiful
diffident = shy (or timid, if you know this word)

dormant (ˈdor·mănt) *adj.* 1. lying asleep or as if asleep, inactive, at rest 2. inactive but capable of becoming active; latent, temporarily quiescent. *The geology students made a surprising discovery: the volcano believed to be dormant was about to erupt.*

droll (drohl) *adj.* amusing in an odd or whimsical way. *This is a wonderful, droll story—the children will love it!*

eclectic (i·ˈklek·tik) *adj.* 1. selecting or employing elements from a variety of sources, systems, or styles 2. consisting of elements from a variety of sources. *You're sure to meet someone interesting at the party—Marieka always invites an eclectic group of people to her gatherings.*

egregious (i·ˈgree·jŭs) *adj.* conspicuously and outrageously bad or offensive; flagrant. *After her egregious accounting error cost the company thousands of dollars, Enid was fired.*

ephemeral (i·'fem·ĕ·răl) *adj.* lasting only a very short time, transitory. *Summer always seems so ephemeral; before you know it, it's time to go back to school again.*

facetious (fă·'see·shŭs) *adj.* humorous and witty, cleverly amusing; jocular, sportive. *Jude's facetious reply angered his teacher but made his classmates laugh.*

fervent ('fur·vent) *adj.* 1. having or showing great emotion; ardent, zealous 2. extremely hot, burning. *Tessie's fervent belief in Omar's innocence sustained him during his years in prison.*

fortuitous (for·'too·i·tŭs) *adj.* happening by accident or chance; occurring unexpectedly or without any known cause. **Note:** *Fortuitous* is commonly used to mean a *happy* accident or an unexpected but *fortunate* occurrence. In its true sense, however, a fortuitous event can be either fortunate or unfortunate. *By a stroke of fortuitous bad luck, Wei chose a small, exclusive resort for her vacation—only to find that the ex-boyfriend she wanted to get away from had also chosen the same resort.*

SHORTCUT: USE WORD PARTS

Remember to use word parts to help you determine and remember meaning. For example, *fervent* has the root *ferv*, which means to boil, bubble, burn. (It is also closely related to *fervid*, a word you know from Chapter 4.) The prefix *im-* in *impervious* means not, and this tells you that *impervious* means *not* pervious.

furtive ('fur·tiv) *adj.* 1. characterized by stealth or secrecy, surreptitious 2. suggesting a hidden motive, shifty. *Harriet's furtive glance told me I had better keep quiet about what I had just seen.*

garrulous ('gar·ŭ·lŭs) *adj.* talkative. *Aunt Midge is as garrulous as they come, so be prepared to listen for hours.*

gregarious (grĕ·'gair·i·ŭs) *adj.* 1. seeking and enjoying the company of others, sociable 2. tending to form a group with others of the same kind. *Since her divorce, Celeste has stopped attending and throwing parties; this goes against her gregarious nature.*

impervious (im·'pur·vi·ŭs) *adj.* 1. incapable of being penetrated 2. not able to be influenced or affected. *Hadley is such a diehard libertarian that he is impervious to any attempts to change his beliefs.*

intrepid (in·'trep·id) *adj.* fearless, brave, undaunted. *Hunger had made the caveman intrepid, and he faced the mammoth without fear.*

latent ('lay·tĕnt) *adj.* present or in existence but not active or evident. *Julian's latent musical talent surfaced when his parents bought an old piano at a garage sale and he started playing.*

lax (laks) *adj.* 1. lacking in rigor or strictness; lenient 2. not taut or rigid; flaccid, slack. *If parents are too lax with their toddlers, chances are they will have a lot of trouble once they enter school, where the children must follow a long list of rules and regulations.*

meticulous (mĕ·'tik·yŭ·lŭs) *adj.* extremely careful and precise; paying great attention to detail. *Tibor was awed by the meticulous detail in the painting—it looked as real as a photograph.*

odious ('oh·di·ŭs) *adj.* contemptible, hateful, detestable. *Zachary found the work in the slaughterhouse so odious that he quit after one day and became a vegetarian.*

paltry ('pawl·tree) *adj.* 1. lacking in importance or worth, insignificant; contemptibly small in amount 2. wretched or contemptible, pitiful. *Walton couldn't believe the billionaire offered such a paltry reward for the return of his lost dog.*

pivotal ('piv·ŏ·tăl) *adj.* being of vital importance, crucial. *We are at a pivotal point in the negotiations and must proceed very carefully; the wrong move now could ruin everything.*

prudent ('proo·dĕnt) *adj.* careful and sensible regarding one's actions and interests; exercising good judgment, judicious. *Clarissa has always been very prudent, so her recent bout of poor choices and boisterous behavior tells me she is very upset about something.*

resplendent (ri·'splen·dĕnt) *adj.* having great splendor or beauty; dazzling, brilliant. *Sanjay stood for a long time on the deck, watching a resplendent sunset over the mountains.*

scintillating ('sin·tĭ·lay·ting) *adj.* 1. sparkling, shining brilliantly 2. brilliantly clever and animated. *I had planned to leave the dinner party early, but the conversation was so scintillating that I stayed until 2:00 in the morning.*

servile ('sur·vīl) *adj.* 1. pertaining to or befitting a slave or forced labor 2. abjectly submissive, slavish. *The climax comes when Yolanda, who had believed she was doomed to play the role of a servile wife to a domineering husband, finds the courage to break the engagement and marry the man she truly loves.*

spurious ('spyoor·i·ŭs) *adj.* false, counterfeit, not genuine or authentic. *Ian's surreptitious manner makes me believe his support for you is spurious and that he has a hidden agenda.*

staunch (stawnch) *adj.* firm and steadfast, unswerving; firm and constant in principle or loyalty. **Note:** As a verb, *stanch* or *staunch* means to stop the flow of blood. *I have always been a staunch believer in the power of positive thinking.*

steadfast ('sted·fast) *adj.* 1. firmly fixed or unchanging, resolute 2. firmly loyal and constant, unswerving. *The captain held a steadfast course despite the rough seas.*

stoic ('stoh·ik) *adj.* seemingly unaffected by pleasure or pain; indifferent, impassive. *Michael's stoic manner is just a façade; underneath he is every bit as emotional as you and I.*

strident ('strī·dĕnt) *adj.* unpleasantly loud and harsh; grating, shrill, discordant. *When he heard the strident tone of his mother's voice, Oscar knew he was in big trouble.*

succinct (sŭk·'singkt) *adj.* expressed clearly and precisely in few words; concise, terse. *Cole's eloquent and succinct essay on the power of positive thinking won first place in the essay contest.*

surreptitious (sur·ĕp·'tish·ŭs) *adj.* 1. done, made, or obtained through stealthy, clandestine, or fraudulent means 2. marked by or acting with stealth or secrecy. *The star-crossed lovers met surreptitiously because their parents did not approve of the relationship.*

timid ('tim·id) *adj.* lacking confidence, conviction, or courage; fearful, hesitant, shy. *Adele was so timid she could barely muster the courage to look another person in the eye.*

vehement ('vee·ĕ·mĕnt) *adj.* 1. characterized by extreme intensity of emotion or forcefulness of expression or conviction 2. marked by great force, vigor, or energy. *The senator vehemently denied any wrongdoing and maintained her innocence throughout the investigation.*

virulent ('vir·yŭ·lĕnt) *adj.* 1. extremely poisonous, injurious or infectious 2. bitterly hostile or hateful, acrimonious. *They say that the pen is mightier than the sword; indeed, words can be every bit as virulent as the sting of a scorpion.*

volatile ('vol·ă·til) *adj.* 1. varying widely, inconstant, changeable, fickle 2. unstable, explosive, likely to change suddenly or violently 3. (in chemistry) evaporating readily. *The stock market has been so volatile lately that I have decided to invest in bonds instead.*

zealous ('zel·ŭs) *adj.* filled with or marked by great interest or enthusiasm; eager, earnest, fervent. *Shalom was such a zealous student that he begged his teacher to assign him extra projects.*

CHEAT SHEET: MIX AND MATCH

To help you remember this grab-bag of important adjectives, match them up in pairs that will help you remember their meaning. For example, *staunch* and *steadfast* have nearly the same meaning; so do *furtive* and *surreptitious*, *dormant* and *latent*, *fervent* and *zealous*, *vehement* and *stoic* and *timid* and *diffident*. On the other hand, *timid* and *intrepid* are opposites, and you could similarly pair *diffident* and *gregarious*. You can also use words from other lessons, too—for example, *garrulous* and *reticent* (from Chapter 4) are also antonyms.

CHEAT SHEET: MORE MNEMONICS

It's advice worth repeating: Take the time to create rhymes, images, or associations that will help you remember the meaning of these adjectives. For example, perhaps you know someone named Tim (or Tina, Tom, Ted, etc.) who is extremely shy. You could use "Timid Tim" (or Tina, Tom, Ted, etc.) to remember what *timid* means. Similarly, you can associate *surreptitious* with a snake. *Surreptitious* begins with the snake's *s* sound and has *repti* in the word, which sounds like *reptile*. Snakes can be very *surreptitious* animals, stealthily sneaking up on their prey.

TIPS AND STRATEGIES

Because adjectives are so important in our communications, you need to be prepared to see a lot of them on your exam. Here are some specific tips and strategies to help you as you prepare for your test.

- Use the context of the sentences provided with the definitions to help you understand these adjectives and memorize their meanings. The sentences help reinforce meaning and convey the words' connotations.
- Pay attention to adjectives as you come across them in your reading, taking special care to note the connotation of the word. One of the main functions of adjectives is to create emotional impact.
- Use synonyms to help you remember meaning, or group words into synonym or antonym pairs. Use words from this chapter and/or other chapters in this book to reinforce what you have already learned.
- Remember to look for familiar prefixes, suffixes, and word roots as you study and use this knowledge to better understand words and determine meaning.
- Watch for words that use the same base as these adjectives. For example, you may not see the word *zealous* on your exam, but you may find *zeal* or *zealot*—and you can accurately guess the meaning of these words by knowing what *zealous* means.
- Remember to use mnemonic devices and associations to help you remember meaning. For example, you might remember *volatile* by associating it with a volcano that is about to erupt.
- Don't forget the power of elimination. Cross out any answers that you know are incorrect and use these other strategies to help you narrow down the remaining choices.

EXTRA HELP

Want to learn more adjectives? Check out Lesson 15 in Learning Express's *Vocabulary and Spelling Success, 3rd edition*, or Chapters 3, 9, 13, 16, 19, and 24 in *501 Vocabulary Questions*. You will find many of these 40 magnificent modifiers within these chapters along with dozens of other practical and commonly tested adjectives.

PRACTICE

By now you have learned and reviewed over 200 words. To help you practice the words in this lesson and review words from earlier in the book, some of the exercises below use vocabulary words from earlier chapters.

For questions 1–15, choose the synonym or antonym as directed.

1. Which word is an **antonym** of *copious*?
   a. abundant
   b. scanty
   c. lax
   d. erratic
   e. severe

2. Which word is a **synonym** of *banal*?
   a. futile
   b. flawed
   c. fortuitous
   d. trite
   e. stealthy

3. Which word is an **antonym** of *pivotal*?
   a. vital
   b. peripheral
   c. pedantic
   d. cryptic
   e. loose

4. Which word is a **synonym** of *garrulous*?
   a. loquacious
   b. fervid
   c. reluctant
   d. wary
   e. supercilious

5. Which word is a **synonym** of *succinct?*
   a. pensive
   b. ingenious
   c. terse
   d. tangential
   e. nominal

6. Which word is an **antonym** of *adroit?*
   a. diligent
   b. apathetic
   c. multifaceted
   d. inept
   e. benign

7. Which word is a **synonym** of *ephemeral?*
   a. transitory
   b. intermittent
   c. circumspect
   d. innocuous
   e. eloquent

8. Which word is an **antonym** of *fervent?*
   a. indifferent
   b. disinterested
   c. caustic
   d. droll
   e. illicit

9. Which word is a **synonym** of *dormant?*
   a. pugnacious
   b. implacable
   c. voluntary
   d. quiescent
   e. lucid

10. Which word is an **antonym** of *lax?*
    a. veritable
    b. destitute
    c. fundamental
    d. cursory
    e. rigorous

11. Which word is an **antonym** of *volatile*?
   a. paltry
   b. steadfast
   c. abysmal
   d. explicit
   e. inscrutable

12. Which word is a **synonym** of *servile*?
   a. eclectic
   b. energetic
   c. submissive
   d. uniform
   e. intrepid

13. Which word is an **antonym** of *virulent*?
   a. innocuous
   b. incontrovertible
   c. violent
   d. excruciating
   e. tedious

14. Which word is a **synonym** of *paltry*?
   a. elusive
   b. lamentable
   c. indolent
   d. regrettable
   e. pungent

15. Which word is a **synonym** of *resplendent*?
   a. droll
   b. dubious
   c. luminous
   d. educational
   e. retroactive

For questions 16–35, choose the answer that best reflects the meaning of the italicized vocabulary word to complete the sentence.

16. An *egregious* error is:
   a. harmless and easily overlooked.
   b. deadly.
   c. caused by many people.
   d. extremely bad.
   e. humorous, laughable.

17. A *meticulous* employee:
    a. is always late.
    b. pays great attention to detail.
    c. deserves a promotion.
    d. receives an extravagant salary.
    e. is careless and sloppy.

18. At a party, a *gregarious* person would:
    a. sit quietly in a corner.
    b. tell crude jokes and offensive anecdotes.
    c. spend most of his time eating and drinking.
    d. meet a lot of people and talk comfortably with others.
    e. argue vehemently with other guests.

19. If a critic calls a new musical *droll*, you should:
    a. buy tickets immediately; it's a spectacular musical.
    b. avoid going at all costs; it's a pathetic production.
    c. get tickets if you like musicals of the whimsical, amusing sort.
    d. get tickets if you like musicals that deal with serious or historical subjects.
    e. bring your children, because the musical is best for younger audiences.

20. If you have a *spurious* coin in your collection, the coin is:
    a. a counterfeit.
    b. extremely valuable.
    c. the only one of its kind.
    d. relatively worthless.
    e. in pristine condition.

21. A *strident* sound is likely to:
    a. lull you to sleep.
    b. make you want to dance.
    c. be very disturbing and annoying.
    d. be caused by a large group of people.
    e. be soothing, pleasant to hear.

22. If someone is described as having a *scintillating* personality, you can expect that person to be:
    a. a genius.
    b. arrogant and disdainful of others.
    c. painfully shy.
    d. brilliantly clever and funny.
    e. outlandish and eccentric.

23. An *austere* room is one that:
   a. is very small, cramped.
   b. is spacious, expansive.
   c. is crowded with fancy furniture, draperies, and knick-knacks.
   d. feels like a prison.
   e. is plain, undecorated.

24. If your new coworker is described as *zealous,* you can expect her to be:
   a. extremely eager and enthusiastic about her work.
   b. extremely talented.
   c. unwilling to do her share.
   d. very opinionated and readily sharing those opinions.
   e. under qualified for the position.

25. A *surreptitious* meeting is:
   a. very dangerous.
   b. highly publicized.
   c. secret, clandestine.
   d. of great political importance.
   e. accidental, occurring by chance.

26. A *facetious* remark is:
   a. tangential, irrelevant.
   b. clever, witty.
   c. grossly offensive.
   d. incisive, profound.
   e. sarcastic, biting.

27. A *staunch* ally:
   a. was a former enemy.
   b. has little to offer.
   c. is not to be trusted.
   d. is firmly loyal.
   e. offers only limited support.

28. An *eclectic* record collection:
   a. includes many different kinds of music from many different artists.
   b. focuses exclusively on one kind of music or one artist.
   c. includes only records that are over 50 years old.
   d. focuses on the early work of various artists.
   e. focuses on music that reflects the dominant culture.

29. If your new roommate were *diffident*, he or she would be:
   a. very nosy.
   b. the opposite of you.
   c. very neat and tidy.
   d. constantly annoying.
   e. very shy.

30. A *vehement* defense would be:
   a. half-hearted.
   b. fiery, passionate.
   c. extremely convincing and effective.
   d. forced and insincere.
   e. low-key, casual, relaxed.

31. A *prudent* decision is:
   a. unwise.
   b. based on insufficient or incorrect information.
   c. made without fear or hesitation.
   d. sensible, reflects good judgment.
   e. made without regard to others.

32. A *fortuitous* event:
   a. is rare, occurs very infrequently.
   b. happens by chance.
   c. is a great celebration.
   d. occurs at regular intervals.
   e. has a profound impact on a large number of people.

33. A *latent* infection:
   a. exists in the body but does not yet show symptoms.
   b. is virulent.
   c. is highly contagious.
   d. cannot be traced to its source.
   e. is not treatable by conventional means.

34. A *stoic* person:
   a. is easily irritated.
   b. lacks self-confidence.
   c. is unsteady or unstable.
   d. changes his or her mind frequently.
   e. shows little emotion.

35. A person who is *impervious* to fear:
   a. seems to be frightened by just about everything.
   b. has a long-standing fear of one person or thing, such as spiders.
   c. seems to be afraid of nothing, intrepid.
   d. has an exaggerated fear of someone or something.
   e. is very timid, lacks courage or conviction.

ANSWERS

1. b. *Copious* means large in number or quantity; abundant, plentiful.

2. d. *Banal* means commonplace, trite; obvious and uninteresting. *Trite* (Chapter 2) means repeated too often, overly familiar through overuse; worn out, hackneyed.

3. b. *Pivotal* means being of vital importance, crucial. *Peripheral* (Chapter 5) means (1) of or relating to the periphery or edge; on the outer boundary; (2) not of central importance or relevance.

4. a. *Garrulous* means talkative. *Loquacious* (Chapter 4) means very talkative, garrulous.

5. c. *Succinct* means expressed clearly and precisely in few words; concise, terse. *Terse* (Chapter 2) means concise, using no unnecessary words, succinct.

6. d. *Adroit* means skillful, clever, or adept in action or in thought; dexterous, deft. *Inept* (Chapter 2) means (1) not suitable, inappropriate; (2) absurd, foolish; (3) incompetent, bungling and clumsy.

7. a. *Ephemeral* means lasting only a very short time, transitory.

8. a. *Fervent* means (1) having or showing great emotion; ardent. *Indifferent* means having no particular interest or concern; apathetic.

9. d. *Dormant* means (1) lying asleep or as if asleep, inactive, at rest; (2) inactive but capable of becoming active; *latent*, temporarily quiescent. *Quiescent* (Chapter 4) means inactive, quiet, at rest; *dormant, latent*.

10. e. *Lax* means (1) lacking in rigor or strictness, lenient; (2) not taut or rigid; flaccid, slack.

11. b. *Volatile* means (1) varying widely, inconstant, changeable, fickle; (2) unstable, explosive, likely to change suddenly or violently. *Steadfast* (this lesson) means (1) firmly fixed and unchanging, resolute; (2) firmly loyal and constant, unswerving.

12. c. *Servile* means (1) pertaining to or befitting a slave or forced labor; (2) abjectly submissive, slavish.

13. a. *Virulent* means (1) extremely poisonous, injurious, or infectious; (2) bitterly hostile or hateful, acrimonious. *Innocuous* (Chapter 4) means harmless, having no adverse or ill effects; not likely to upset or offend.

14. b. *Paltry* means (1) lacking in importance or worth, insignificant; contemptibly small in amount; (2) wretched or contemptible, pitiful. *Lamentable* (Chapter 3) means (1) regrettable, unfortunate; inspiring grief or mourning; (2) deplorable, pitiable.

15. c. *Resplendent* means having great splendor or beauty; dazzling, brilliant. *Luminous* (Chapter 4) means shining, emitting light; full of light, bright, brilliant.

16. d. *Egregious* means conspicuously and outrageously bad or offensive; flagrant.

17. b. *Meticulous* means extremely careful and precise; paying great attention to detail.

18. d. *Gregarious* means (1) seeking and enjoying the company of others, sociable; (2) tending to form a group with others of the same kind.

19. c. *Droll* means amusing in an odd or whimsical way.

20. a. *Spurious* means false, counterfeit, not genuine or authentic.

21. c. *Strident* means unpleasantly loud and harsh; grating, shrill, discordant.

22. d. *Scintillating* means (1) sparkling, shining brilliantly; (2) brilliantly clever and animated.

23. e. *Austere* means (1) severe or stern in attitude or appearance; (2) simple, unadorned, very plain.

24. a. *Zealous* means filled with or marked by great interest or enthusiasm; eager, earnest, fervent.

25. c. *Surreptitious* means (1) done, made, or obtained through stealthy, clandestine, or fraudulent means; (2) marked by or acting with stealth or secrecy.

26. b. *Facetious* means humorous and witty, cleverly amusing; jocular, sportive.

27. d. *Staunch* means firm and steadfast, unswerving; firm and constant in principle or loyalty.

28. a. *Eclectic* means (1) selecting or employing elements from a variety of sources, systems, or styles; (2) consisting of elements from a variety of sources.

29. e. *Diffident* means lacking self-confidence, shy and timid.

30. b. *Vehement* means (1) characterized by extreme intensity of emotion or forcefulness of expression or conviction; (2) marked by great force, vigor, or energy.

31. d. *Prudent* means careful and sensible regarding one's actions and interests; exercising good judgment, judicious.

32. b. *Fortuitous* means happening by accident or chance; occurring unexpectedly or without any known cause.

33. a. *Latent* means present or in existence but not active or evident.

34. e. *Stoic* means seemingly unaffected by pleasure or pain; indifferent, impassive.

35. c. *Impervious* means (1) incapable of being penetrated; (2) not able to be influenced or affected.

Versatile Verbs

While your vocabulary test is sure to be loaded with adjectives, there's no doubt that you will also see plenty of verbs—the fundamental building block of sentences. Before you begin learning and reviewing versatile verbs, take a few minutes to take this ten-question *Benchmark Quiz*. These questions are similar to the type of questions that you will find on important tests. When you are finished, check the answer key carefully to assess your results. Your Benchmark Quiz analysis will help you determine how much time you need to spend on reviewing verbs as well as the specific words you need to learn in order to increase your vocabulary power. This chapter presents 35 versatile verbs to help you broaden your word base and improve your score on the exam.

BENCHMARK QUIZ

Choose the answer that best expresses the meaning of the italicized word to complete the sentence.

1. To *abhor* something is to:
   a. appreciate it.
   b. value it.
   c. despise it.
   d. intensify it.
   e. encircle it.

2. If you *daunt* someone, you:
   a. offend that person.
   b. intimidate that person.
   c. accuse that person.
   d. injure that person.
   e. criticize that person.

3. If you *sanction* something, you:
   a. authorize it.
   b. apply for it.
   c. cleanse it.
   d. damage it.
   e. scatter it.

4. Something that *ebbs:*
   a. deceives.
   b. reconciles.
   c. strengthens.
   d. recedes.
   e. opposes.

5. To *purge* something is to:
   a. expand it.
   b. diminish it.
   c. avoid it.
   d. admire it.
   e. cleanse it.

6. To *detract* means to:
   a. to stubbornly refuse.
   b. to draw or take away from.
   c. to make certain, confirm.
   d. to fix firmly and securely.
   e. to regard with contempt or scorn.

7. To *meander* is to:
   a. wander about aimlessly.
   b. spread everywhere.
   c. ask for, petition.
   d. regard with awe.
   e. take by force.

8. If you *appease* someone, you:
   a. attack that person.
   b. accuse that person of an unlawful act.
   c. deceive that person.
   d. pacify that person.
   e. give praise to that person.

9. If you *disdain* someone, you:
   a. scorn that person.
   b. imitate that person.
   c. distrust that person.
   d. feel indebted to that person.
   e. think highly that person.

10. If two people are *vying*, they are:
    a. arguing.
    b. competing.
    c. collaborating.
    d. conspiring.
    e. embarking.

BENCHMARK QUIZ SOLUTIONS

How did you do on identifying versatile verbs? Check your answers here, and then analyze the results to figure out your plan of action for mastering this topic.

▶ *Answers*

1. c. To *abhor* means to regard with horror or repugnance, detest.

2. b. To *daunt* means to intimidate, to make afraid or discouraged.

3. a. To *sanction* is to approve or permit; to give official authorization or approval for.

4. d. To *ebb* is to flow back or recede, as the tide; to fall back, decline.

5. e. To *purge* means to free from impurities, especially to rid of that which is undesirable or harmful; to make or become clean, pure.

6. b. To *detract* is to draw or take away from; to remove part of something, diminish.

7. a. To *meander* is move on a winding or turning course; to wander about, move aimlessly or without a fixed direction or course.

8. d. To *appease* means to make calm or quiet, soothe; to still or pacify.

9. a. To *disdain* is to regard with haughty contempt or scorn, despise; to consider or reject as unworthy or beneath one's dignity.

10. b. To *vie* is to compete with or contend; to strive for superiority or victory.

BENCHMARK QUIZ RESULTS

If you answered 8–10 questions correctly, well done! You are already familiar with many of these versatile verbs. Give the lesson a quick review and do the practice exercise. If your score on the practice test is equally high, move on to Chapter 9.

If you answered 4–7 questions correctly, you already know some of these important vocabulary words, but you need more of these versatile verbs in your permanent vocabulary. Be sure to set aside some time to carefully review the verbs listed in this chapter.

If you answered 1–3 questions correctly, it's time to expand the number of verbs in your vocabulary and add some more sophisticated action words to your word base. Study the lesson that follows carefully, and do the practice quiz on a separate sheet of paper so that you can do the exercise several times if necessary. See the source listed in **Extra Help** for more review and practice.

JUST IN TIME LESSON—VERSATILE VERBS

Lights, camera, and . . . ACTION! When it comes to parts of speech, the verb, as they say, is king. Verbs express an action or state of being: *to go, to run, to exclaim, to mediate; to desire, to believe, to doubt, to anticipate.* They are part of every communication. Our most common one-word sentences are verb commands: *Go! Stop! Wait! Hurry! Smile!* Even in one-word sentences such as *Yes* or *Tomorrow*, the verb is implied or understood:

> "Do you understand?"
> "Yes (I *do*)."

> "When will you return?"
> "(I *will return*) tomorrow."

Verbs always have a **subject**, the person or thing performing the action or existing in a particular state of being. Thus, verbs tell us what the subject **is** or **does**:

> Hassan *is* hungry.
> Emilie *wondered* where Kahlid *had gone*.
> Rich *rectified* the situation.
> Her mannerisms *remind* me of my grandmother.

Because of their essential function, verbs are a particularly powerful part of speech, and the right verb can have tremendous impact. Notice for example how much more precise and powerful the following sentence becomes when the right verb is used:

> Rachel really *looks up* to her aunt.
> Rachel really *respects* her aunt.
> Rachel *reveres* her aunt.

To *revere* means to regard with reverence or awe; to venerate. It is much more powerful than *respect* because it conveys a sense of awe and inspiration, suggesting that one being revered is honorable, stately, even sacred. Because it is so strong, the sentence no longer needs the word *really* to express degree. Here is another example:

Lester loves to fish, but he *can't stand* seafood.
Lester loves to fish, but he *despises* seafood.
Lester loves to fish, but he *abhors* seafood.

To *abhor* means to regard with horror or repugnance, detest. It is a much stronger word than *despise* because it connotes a hate so strong it sickens or disgusts.

The broader your word base, the more precisely you will be able to describe an action or state of being, and the more easily you will be able to choose a verb that conveys exactly the meaning and connotation you wish to convey. The 35 verbs defined below appear frequently on vocabulary exams, but you can also expect to encounter them regularly in your day to day communications. Each definition includes a sample sentence to show you the verb in context. Learn these verbs well to improve your test score, to understand more of what you read, and to more accurately express what people are and do.

WORD LIST

abate (ă·'bayt) *v.* to lessen in strength, intensity, or degree; subside. *As the violent storm abated, we began to survey the damage it caused.*

abhor (ab·'hohr) *v.* to regard with horror or repugnance, detest. *I know Carlos abhors politics, but he should still get out and vote.*

appease (ă·'peez) *v.* to make calm or quiet, soothe; to still or pacify. *The only way to appease Lawrence is to concede that he is right.*

augment (awg·'ment) *v.* to increase in size, strength, or intensity; enlarge. *Arty tried to help Ann and Stan settle their differences, but his interference only augmented the problem.*

balk (bawk) *v.* 1. to stop abruptly and refuse to go on 2. to obstinately refuse or oppose. *Old man Jones was finally ready to capitulate and sell his land to the timber company, but he balked when he saw that he would only be compensated for half of the value of his property.*

cajole (kă·'johl) *v.* to urge with gentle and repeated appeals or flattery; to wheedle. *Valerie is quite adept at cajoling others to get what she wants, even if it's something she hasn't earned.*

capitulate (kă·'pich·ŭ·layt) *v.* to surrender under specific terms or agreed upon conditions; to give in, acquiesce. *The editor refused to capitulate to the demands of the sales team because she wanted to uphold her high grammatical standards.*

corroborate (kŏ·'rob·ŏ·rayt) *v.* to strengthen or support with evidence or authority; to make more certain, confirm. *Both Irma's and Ye's statements corroborate Tia's story, so she must be telling the truth.*

daunt (dawnt) *v.* to intimidate, to make afraid or discouraged. *Don't be daunted by Holden's austere manner; he's really a very kind and understanding person.*

detract (di·'trakt) *v.* to draw or take away from; to remove part of something, diminish. *Unfortunately, Helen's slovenly appearance detracted from the impact of her otherwise brilliant presentation.*

SHORTCUT: MNEMONICS AGAIN . . . AND AGAIN . . . AND AGAIN . . .

It's worth repeating yet again: As you prepare for your exam, take the time to create rhymes, images, or associations that will help you remember the meaning of these verbs. For example, you might associate *ensconce* with a <u>sconce</u> that you hang (fix securely) on the wall. *Abhor* means to regard with <u>hor</u>ror or repugnance; this similarity can help you remember its meaning. A <u>gird</u>le is something that *girds*—it encircles or binds, encompasses.

disdain (dis·'dayn) *v.* 1. to regard with haughty contempt or scorn, despise 2. to consider or reject (someone or something) as unworthy or beneath one's dignity. **Note:** *Disdain (n.)* means a feeling or showing of haughty contempt or scorn; a state of being despised. *I was humiliated by the way Angelica disdained every idea I proposed at that meeting.*

dissipate ('dis·ĭ·payt) *v.* 1. to separate and scatter completely; to disperse to the point of disappearing, or nearly so 2. to be extravagant and wasteful, especially in the pursuit of pleasure; squander. *The crowd dissipated when the riot police arrived, and only the very angriest protesters remained.*

dupe (doop) *v.* to deceive, trick. **Note:** A *dupe (n.)* is someone who is easily deceived, gullible. *Charlene was duped into buying this lemon of a car by a slick·talking salesman.*

ebb (eb) *v.* 1. to flow back or recede, as the tide 2. to fall back, decline. *I hope Mark's anger has ebbed; I am eager for a reconciliation.*

enscance (en·'skons) *v.* 1. to fix or settle firmly and securely 2. to place or hide securely, conceal. *Once the spy was comfortably ensconced in his new identity, he began his secret mission.*

gird (gurd) *v.* 1. to encircle or bind with a belt or band 2. to encompass, surround 3. to prepare for action, especially military confrontation 4. to sneer at, mock, gibe. *The negotiations had failed, and the soldiers girded for battle.*

grovel ('gruv·ĕl) *v.* to lie or creep with one's face to the ground in a servile, humble, or fearful manner. *Panji, if you want your boss to treat you with respect, you've got to stop groveling and stand up for yourself.*

languish ('lang·gwish) *v.* 1. to lose vigor or strength; to become languid, feeble, weak 2. to exist or continue in a miserable or neglected state. *Lucinda languished in despair when Sven told her he'd fallen in love with another woman.*

maim (maym) *v.* to wound, cripple, or injure, especially by depriving of the use of a limb or other part of the body; to mutilate, disfigure, disable. *The mining accident left Antol alive but severely maimed.*

SHORTCUT: USE WORD PARTS

Once again, remember to use word parts to help you learn and remember meaning. For example, *detract* uses the prefix *de-*, meaning down, from, away. Hence its meaning: to draw or take away from; to remove part of something, diminish. *Disdain* and *dissipate* both begin with the prefix *dis-*, meaning away from, apart, reversal, not. Thus, their respective meanings: (1) to regard with haughty contempt or scorn, despise; to consider or reject (someone or something) as unworthy or beneath one's dignity; and (2) to separate and scatter completely; to disperse to the point of disappearing, or nearly so. Similarly, *rescind* uses the prefix *re-*, meaning back or again. Hence its meaning: to repeal or cancel; to void or annul.

mar (mahr) *v.* 1. to impair or damage, make defective or imperfect 2. to spoil the perfection or integrity of. *The strident sounds of Omar's abysmal saxophone playing marred the serenity of the afternoon.*

meander (mee·'an·dĕr) *v.* 1. to move on a winding or turning course 2. to wander about, move aimlessly or without a fixed direction or course. *I meandered through the park for hours, trying to figure out how I could have made such an egregious mistake.*

mitigate ('mit·ĭ·gayt) *v.* 1. to make less intense or severe 2. to moderate the force or intensity of, soften, diminish, alleviate. *I am sure that if you tell the headmaster the truth, the extenuating circumstances will mitigate the severity of your punishment.*

pervade (pĕr·'vayd) *v.* to spread everywhere, permeate; to be diffused or present throughout. *Fear pervaded the classroom after Sally started a rumor that Mr. Higgins would be their new teacher.*

purge (purj) *v.* to free from impurities, especially to rid of that which is undesirable or harmful; to make or become clean, pure. *After Leon writes a draft, he purges the text of unnecessary words to make it more succinct.*

rebuke (ri·'byook) *v.* 1. to criticize sharply; to reprove or reprimand, censure 2. to repress or restrain by expressing harsh disapproval. *After weeks of being rebuked in front of his coworkers for minor infractions and imaginary offenses, Ameer realized he was being persecuted by his boss.*

rescind (ri·'sind) *v.* to repeal or cancel; to void or annul. *The Olsens rescinded their offer to buy the house when they discovered the property was in a flood zone.*

revere (ri·'veer) *v.* to regard with reverence or awe; to venerate, hold in highest respect or estimation. *When you look at Judith's work, it's easy to see which painter she reveres most; every painting is an homage to Cezanne.*

roil (roil) *v.* 1. to make a liquid cloudy or muddy 2. to stir up or agitate 3. to anger or annoy. *The crowd was roiled by the speaker's insensitive remarks.*

sanction ('sangk·shŏn) *v.* 1. to approve or permit; to give official authorization or approval for, ratify. **Note:** The noun *sanction* means (1) official authorization or approval (2) a penalty imposed to coerce another to comply or conform. *The city council has sanctioned our request to turn the empty lot into a community garden.*

solicit (sŏ·'lis·it) *v.* 1. to ask for earnestly, petition 2. to seek to obtain by persuasion or formal application 3. to approach with an offer for paid sexual services. *Cy was touting the merits of the referendum as he solicited support for Tuesday's vote.*

CHEAT SHEET: MIX AND MATCH SENTENCES

To help you remember these important verbs *and* to review the wonderful adjectives from Chapter 7, match verbs and adjectives together in pairs that will help you recall their meaning. Here are several examples:

- You *abhor* what is *odious.*
- You might *disdain* something that is *banal.*
- You won't be *daunted* if you are *intrepid;* you will be *daunted* if you are *timid.*
- You might *tout* something about which you are *fervent.*
- You might *vacillate* if you are *timid* or *diffident.*
- You might *grovel* if you are *servile.*

You can also mix and match words from this and other chapters to create synonym and antonym pairs. *Abate* and *ebb,* for example, have nearly the same meaning, while *disdain* and *revere* are opposites.

tout (towt) *v.* 1. to promote or praise highly and energetically, especially with the goal of getting a customer, vote, etc. 2. to solicit (customers, votes, etc.) in an especially brazen or persistent manner. *Genevieve touted her eye cream as a wonder product because it removed her wrinkles after just ten weeks.*

usurp (yoo·'surp) *v.* to seize, take possession of, by force and without right; to wrongfully take over. *After the king's half-brother usurped the throne, he executed the king and queen and imprisoned the prince, who was the rightful heir to the throne.*

vacillate ('vas·ĭ·layt) *v.* 1. to move or sway from side to side, fluctuate 2. to swing back and forth about an opinion, course of action, etc.; to be indecisive, waver. *Denise vacillated for weeks before she decided to accept our offer.*

vie (vī) *v.* to compete with or contend; to strive for superiority or victory. *The two scientists were vying to be the first to find concrete evidence of extraterrestrial life.*

winnow ('win·oh) *v.* 1. to separate the grain from the chaff by using the wind or other current of air to blow the chaff away 2. to separate the good from the bad; to examine or sift through to remove undesirable elements. *We have winnowed the list of applicants down to five highly-qualified candidates.*

CHEAT SHEET: A MATTER OF DEGREE

As you learn and review these verbs, be sure to read the definitions and sample sentences carefully to note their denotations and connotations. Many verbs are similar in meaning but are differentiated by degree. For example, *maim* and *mar* have similar meanings, but *maim* is more severe than *mar*. To *dissipate* is stronger (more complete a disappearance) than to *disperse* (Chapter 6).

TIPS AND STRATEGIES

No sentence is complete without a verb, and you can expect to see a lot of verbs on your exam. Here are some specific tips and strategies to help you as you prepare for your test.

- Use the context of the sentences provided with the definitions to help you understand these verbs and memorize their meanings. The sentences help reinforce meaning and convey the words' connotations.
- Pay attention to verbs as you come across them in your reading, taking special care to note their contexts and connotations.
- Use synonyms to help you remember meaning, or group words into synonym or antonym pairs. Use words from this chapter and/or other chapters in this book to reinforce what you have already learned.
- Remember to look for familiar prefixes, suffixes, and word roots as you study and use this knowledge to better understand words and determine meaning.
- Watch for words that use the same base as these verbs. For example, you may see the word *pervasive* on your exam. If you know what *pervade* means, you can determine the meaning of its adjective form.

- Use mnemonic devices and associations to help you remember meaning. For example, you might remember *revere* by associating it with Paul Revere, a revered figure in the history of the American Revolution.
- Don't forget the power of elimination. Cross out any answers that you know are incorrect and use these other strategies to help you narrow down the remaining choices.

EXTRA HELP

Want to learn more verbs? Check out Chapters 5 and 14 in Learning-Express's *501 Vocabulary Questions*. You will find several of the 35 vivid verbs within these chapters along with dozens of other practical and commonly tested verbs.

PRACTICE

To help you practice the words in this lesson and review words from earlier in this book, some of the exercises below use vocabulary words from earlier chapters.

For questions 1–10, choose the best **synonym** for each vocabulary word.

1. gird
   a. refine
   b. wind
   c. ratify
   d. encircle
   e. fluctuate

2. maim
   a. cripple
   b. intensify
   c. agitate
   d. seize
   e. surrender

3. rescind
   a. replicate
   b. permeate
   c. repeal
   d. waver
   e. conceal

4. dupe
  a. duplicate
  b. destroy
  c. scatter
  d. deceive
  e. promote

5. vacillate
  a. fluctuate
  b. intimidate
  c. oppose
  d. soothe
  e. subside

6. cajole
  a. support
  b. wheedle
  c. squander
  d. humiliate
  e. discourage

7. rebuke
  a. defeat
  b. embellish
  c. censure
  d. undermine
  e. thwart

8. capitulate
  a. acquiesce
  b. subjugate
  c. undermine
  d. allocate
  e. rectify

9. revere
  a. abscond
  b. equivocate
  c. evade
  d. teem
  e. venerate

10. appease
   a. emulate
   b. castigate
   c. placate
   d. elude
   e. hoard

For questions 11–20, choose the best **antonym** for each vocabulary word.

11. sanction
   a. release
   b. forbid
   c. praise
   d. enjoin
   e. refuse

12. purge
   a. reduce
   b. entice
   c. permeate
   b. defile
   e. ridicule

13. abhor
   a. hinder
   b. relinquish
   c. wander
   d. reject
   e. adore

14. daunt
   a. recede
   b. encourage
   c. enlighten
   d. frighten
   e. entertain

15. abate
   a. intensify
   b. regulate
   c. damage
   d. beg
   e. weaken

16. disdain
   a. pique
   b. condescend
   c. revere
   d. surmise
   e. pervade

17. dissipate
   a. tout
   b. digress
   c. presage
   d. juxtapose
   e. coalesce

18. mitigate
   a. diffuse
   b. exacerbate
   c. indict
   d. deluge
   e. persecute

19. roil
   a. appease
   b. teem
   c. vie
   d. garner
   e. discern

20. augment
   a. winnow
   b. hone
   c. detract
   d. meander
   e. incense

For questions 21–35, choose the vocabulary word that best completes the sentence.

21. The bill _____ in committees for months, and we began to lose hope that it would ever be passed.
    a. balked
    b. ebbed
    c. roiled
    d. languished
    e. winnowed

22. Chester _____ before his girlfriend—or rather, his ex-girlfriend—hoping that his humility would win her back.
    a. groveled
    b. touted
    c. appeased
    d. ensconced
    e. revered

23. I am tired of constantly _____ for his attention; he is always so pre-occupied with work.
    a. soliciting
    b. languishing
    c. corroborating
    d. vying
    e. dissipating

24. By the way he was _____ his business, I could tell he was desperate for customers.
    a. usurping
    b. disdaining
    c. touting
    d. girding
    e. rebuking

25. Jonie had always wanted to go skydiving, but she _____ when she was actually up in a plane and would not jump.
    a. balked
    b. stooped
    c. marred
    d. daunted
    e. duped

26. I have come to _____ your support for my candidacy.
  a. augment
  b. corroborate
  c. cajole
  d. solicit
  e. tout

27. It took days for the programmers to _____ out the errors in the program, but once they did, it worked beautifully.
  a. dissipate
  b. capitulate
  c. detract
  d. rescind
  e. winnow

28. Ian's political fervor will _____ now that his favorite candidate has been eliminated in the primary.
  a. abhor
  b. appease
  c. ebb
  d. rescind
  e. detract

29. The witnesses' accounts all _____ the defendant's story.
  a. augmented
  b. corroborated
  c. mitigated
  d. marred
  e. girded

30. Since you lied to me, an atmosphere of distrust has _____ our entire relationship.
  a. detracted
  b. sanctioned
  c. pervaded
  d. languished
  e. abhorred

31. The exquisite vase was _____ by a small crack on its handle.
  a. maimed
  b. purged
  c. winnowed
  d. ensconced
  e. marred

32. The rebels _____ the village and stole freely from the villagers' homes.
    a. rescinded
    b. cajoled
    c. capitulated
    d. usurped
    e. roiled

33. The hidden camera was safely _____ in the picture frame.
    a. abated
    b. ensconced
    c. girded
    d. duped
    e. winnowed

34. The river _____ through the valley.
    a. groveled
    b. balked
    c. meandered
    d. ebbed
    e. pervaded

35. Yuri did his best to _____ me, but I would not let him intimidate me.
    a. cajole
    b. roil
    c. solicit
    d. daunt
    e. dupe

ANSWERS

1. d. To *gird* means to (1) encircle or bind with a belt or band; (2) encompass, surround; (3) prepare for action, especially military confrontation; (4) sneer at, mock, gibe.

2. a. To *maim* means to wound, cripple, or injure, especially by depriving of the use of a limb or other part of the body; to mutilate, disfigure, disable.

3. c. To *rescind* is to repeal or cancel; to void or annul.

4. d. To *dupe* is to deceive, trick.

5. a. To *vacillate* means (1) to move or sway from side to side, fluctuate; (2) to swing back and forth about an opinion, course of action, etc.; to be indecisive, waver.

6. b. To *cajole* means to urge with gentle and repeated appeals or flattery; wheedle.

7. c. To *rebuke* means (1) to criticize sharply; to reprove or reprimand, censure; (2) to repress or restrain by expressing harsh disapproval.

8. a. To *capitulate* is to surrender under specific terms or agreed upon conditions; to give in, acquiesce.

9. e. To *revere* means to regard with reverence or awe; to venerate, hold in highest respect or estimation.

10. c. To *appease* is to make calm or quiet, soothe; to still or pacify.

11. b. To *sanction* means (1) to approve or permit; (2) to give official authorization or approval for, ratify.

12. d. To *purge* is to free from impurities, especially to rid of that which is undesirable or harmful; to make or become clean, pure.

13. e. To *abhor* is to regard with horror or repugnance, detest.

14. b. To *daunt* is to intimidate, to make afraid or discouraged.

15. a. To *abate* is to lessen in strength, intensity, or degree; subside.

16. c. To *disdain* means (1) to regard with haughty contempt or scorn, despise; (2) to consider or reject as unworthy or beneath one's dignity.

17. e. To *dissipate* means (1) to separate and scatter completely; to disperse to the point of disappearing, or nearly so; (2) to be extravagant and wasteful, especially in the pursuit of pleasure; squander.

18. b. To *mitigate* means (1) to make les intense or severe; (2) to moderate the force or intensity of, soften, diminish, alleviate.

19. a. To *roil* means (1) to make a liquid cloudy or muddy; (2) to stir up or agitate; (3) to anger or annoy.

20. c. To *augment* is to increase in size, strength, or intensity; enlarge.

21. d. To *languish* means (1) to lose vigor or strength; to become languid, feeble, weak; (2) to exist or continue in a miserable or neglected state. This sentence uses the second meaning.

22. a. To *grovel* means to lie or creep with one's face to the ground in a servile, humble, or fearful manner.

23. d. To *vie* means to compete with or contend; to strive for superiority or victory.

24. c. To *tout* means (1) to promote or praise highly and energetically, especially with the goal of getting a customer, vote, etc.; (2) to solicit (customers, votes, etc.) in an especially brazen or persistent manner. This sentence can use either meaning.

25. a. To *balk* means (1) to stop abruptly and refuse to go on; (2) to obstinately refuse or oppose. This sentence uses primarily the first meaning.

26. d. To *solicit* means (1) to ask for earnestly, petition; (2) to seek to obtain by persuasion or formal application; (3) to approach with an offer for paid sexual services. This sentence can use the first or second meaning.

27. e. To *winnow* means (1) to separate the grain from the chaff by using the wind or other current of air to blow the chaff away; (2) to separate the good from the bad; to examine or sift through to remove undesirable elements. This sentence uses the second meaning.

28. c. To *ebb* means (1) to flow back or recede, as the tide; (2) to fall back, decline. This sentence uses primarily the second meaning.

29. b. To *corroborate* means to strengthen or support with evidence or authority; to make more certain, confirm.

30. c. To *pervade* is to spread everywhere, permeate; to be diffused or present throughout.

31. e. To *mar* means (1) to impair or damage, make defective or imperfect; (2) to spoil the perfection or integrity of. The context clue *small crack* indicates that *mar* is the appropriate word, not *maim*.

32. d. To *usurp* is to seize, take possession of, by force and without right; to wrongfully take over.

33. b. To *ensconce* means (1) to fix or settle firmly and securely; (2) to place or hide securely, conceal. This sentence uses the second meaning.

34. c. To *meander* means (1) to move on a winding or turning course; (2) to wander about, move aimlessly or without a fixed direction or course.

35. d. To *daunt* is to intimidate, to make afraid or discouraged.

Foreign Words and Phrases

If foreign words and phrases are all Greek to you, then this chapter will be especially helpful. Many foreign terms are regularly used in English communications, and you should be familiar with some of the most common foreign words and phrases for your exam. Before you begin learning and reviewing versatile verbs, take a few minutes to take this ten-question *Benchmark Quiz*. These questions are similar to the type of questions that you will find on important tests. When you are finished, check the answer key carefully to assess your results. Your Benchmark Quiz analysis will help you determine how much time you need to spend on reviewing foreign words as well as the specific words you need to learn in order to increase your vocabulary power. This chapter presents 35 foreign terms for your review.

BENCHMARK QUIZ

Choose the word whose definition best matches the description.

1. an innovative play that uses an experimental style
   a. apropos
   b. mélange
   c. avant-garde
   d. imbroglio
   e. vignette

2. the complete works of Shakespeare
   a. blasé
   b. milieu
   c. zeitgeist
   d. parvenu
   e. oeuvre

3. a meeting at 7:00 at La Grange restaurant
   a. par excellence
   b. rendezvous
   c. savoir faire
   d. façade
   e. debut

4. "work like a dog," "sleep like a baby," and other such overused sayings
   a. cliché
   b. bourgeois
   c. insouciant
   d. gauche
   e. ennui

5. an avid sports fan
   a. gestalt
   b. hiatus
   c. mélange
   d. epitome
   e. aficionado

6. an artist's first gallery showing
   a. ennui
   b. imbroglio
   c. parvenu
   d. debut
   e. façade

7. a temporary separation in a relationship
   a. blasé
   b. quid pro quo
   c. hiatus
   d. malaise
   e. liaison

8. a world-renowned celebrity wearing a disguise
   a. incognito
   b. imbroglio
   c. milieu
   d. oeuvre
   e. rendezvous

9. pretending not to be hurt by an insulting remark
   a. ad hoc
   b. gauche
   c. cliché
   d. façade
   e. gestalt

10. someone who reports students' questions and concerns to the dean
    a. aficionado
    b. liaison
    c. parvenu
    d. vis-à-vis
    e. epitome

BENCHMARK QUIZ SOLUTIONS

How did you do on identifying foreign words? Check your answers here, and then analyze the results to figure out your plan of attack for mastering this topic.

▶ *Answers*

1. **c.** *Avant-garde* means using or favoring an ultramodern or experimental style; innovative, cutting-edge, especially in the arts or literature.

2. **e.** *Oeuvre* means (1) a work of art; (2) the total lifework of a writer, artist, composer, etc.

3. **b.** The noun *rendezvous* means (1) a prearranged meeting at a certain time and place; (2) a place where people meet, especially a popular gathering place. The verb *rendezvous* means to bring or come together at a certain place, to meet at a rendezvous.

4. **a.** A *cliché* is a trite or overused expression or idea.

5. **e.** An *aficionado* is a fan or devotee, especially of a sport or pastime.

6. **d.** A *debut* is a first appearance in or presentation to the public.

7. **c.** *Hiatus* means a gap or opening; an interruption or break.

8. **a.** *Incognito* means with one's identity concealed; in disguise or under an assumed character or identity.

9. **d.** A *façade* is (1) the face or front of a building; (2) an artificial or deceptive front, especially one intended to hide something unpleasant.

10. **b.** *Liaison* means (1) a channel or means of connection or communication between two groups; one who maintains such communication; (2) a close relationship or link, especially one that is secretive or adulterous.

BENCHMARK QUIZ RESULTS

If you answered 8–10 questions correctly, well done! You are already familiar with many of these foreign words and phrases. Give the lesson a quick review and do the practice exercise. If your score on the practice test is equally high, move on to Chapter 10.

If you answered 4–7 questions correctly, you already know some of these important foreign words and phrases, but you need more of these commonly tested terms in your permanent vocabulary. Be sure to set aside some time to carefully review the vocabulary words listed in this chapter.

If you answered 1–3 questions correctly, it's time to expand the number of foreign words and phrases in your vocabulary. Study the lesson that follows carefully, and do the practice quiz on a separate sheet of paper so that you can do the exercise several times if necessary. See the source listed in **Extra Help** for more review and practice.

JUST IN TIME LESSON—FOREIGN WORDS

Unlike business, legal, or technical terms, which tend to appear in specific contexts, the foreign words and phrases you are about to review can appear in any context and have become part of our general English vocabulary. Indeed, the more global our society becomes, the more foreign words and phrases find their way into everyday use in the English language, and the more important it is to learn these words and their meanings.

Many of the foreign words and phrases in this chapter have been adopted into the English language because there are no English words that express exactly the same meaning. No single English word, for example, expresses the same idea as *ad hoc*, which means for a specific, often temporary, purpose; for this case only. To convey the same idea in English, you would need at least three or four words. Other foreign words listed here may have English counterparts but have become part of our language because of their particular connotation or stylistic flair. The French word *gauche*, for example, is similar to the English word *uncouth*, but *gauche* is different enough in sound and sense to warrant its inclusion and use in our language:

> *gauche:* 1. lacking social graces or polish; without tact 2. clumsy or awkward
> *uncouth:* 1. crude, unrefined, lacking cultivation or taste 2. awkward, clumsy, ungraceful

Similarly, another French word, *insouciant*, also has an English synonym, but again, the foreign word carries a slightly different connotation and flavor:

> *insouciant:* blithely unconcerned or carefree; nonchalant, indifferent
> *nonchalant:* indifferent or cool, not showing anxiety or excitement

Insouciant, by the way, comes from the Old French verb *soucier*, meaning to trouble, and the prefix *in-*, meaning not. *Nonchalant* is also a French word, but it was adopted into the English language nearly two centuries ago and therefore has lost its foreign flavor.

The 35 foreign words and phrases defined in this chapter come from the French, Italian, German, Latin, and Greek languages. Because they are used so frequently in everyday English communications, you can expect to encounter many of them on your exam. Each definition includes a sample sentence to show how the word or phrase is used in context. Learn these foreign terms well to improve your test score, to understand more of what you read, and to more accurately express yourself in your day-to-day communications.

Note: As you study these words, be sure to pay extra attention to their spellings—many words have tricky vowel combinations—and their pronunciations. Because they are foreign words, you cannot be sure you are pronouncing them correctly simply by sounding them out. Be sure to say the words out loud as you memorize their meanings.

WORD LIST

ad hoc (ad·ʹhok) *adj.* for a specific, often temporary, purpose; for this case only. *An ad hoc committee will be formed to investigate Stella's allegations.*

aficionado (a·fish·yŏ·ʹnah·doh) *n.* a fan or devotee, especially of a sport or pastime. *Sal is such a Bruce Springsteen aficionado that he bought tickets to all ten Giants Stadium concerts.*

apropos (ap·rŏ·ʹpoh) *adj.* appropriate to the situation; suitable to what is being said or done; *adv.* 1. by the way, incidentally 2. at an appropriate or opportune time. *Chancey's comments may have been disturbing, but they were definitely apropos.*

avant-garde (a·vahnt·ʹgahrd) *adj.* using or favoring an ultramodern or experimental style; innovative, cutting-edge, especially in the arts or literature. *Yvette prefers the avant-garde style of writers like Donald Barthelme to the traditional narrative technique.*

blasé (blah·ʹzay) *adj.* 1. uninterested because of frequent exposure or indulgence 2. nonchalant, unconcerned 3. very sophisticated. *Quincy has traveled so much that he speaks of exotic places such as Borneo in a totally blasé manner.*

bourgeois (boor·zhwah) *adj.* typical of the middle class; conforming to the standards and conventions of the middle class; hence also, commonplace, conservative, or materialistic. *Although she won millions in the lottery, Ada still maintains her bourgeois lifestyle.*

cliché (klee·ʹshay) *n.* a trite or overused expression or idea. *Tito has an original and engaging writing style, but his storylines are such clichés.*

debut (day·ʹbyoo) *n.* a first appearance in or presentation to the public. *Irina's Carnegie Hall debut received rave reviews.*

RULE BOOK: SAY IT AGAIN, SAM

It's important to know how to pronounce any word that you plan to add to your vocabulary, and it's especially important to do so if you are dealing with a foreign word or phrase. So say each word aloud several times as you study. Once you pronounce it, you may realize that you are already familiar with that term.

de facto (dee·ˈfak·toh) *adj.* in reality or fact; actual. *The king is only the nominal head of the country; the de facto leader is the prime minister.*

ennui (ahn·ˈwee) *n.* boredom and listlessness resulting from something tedious or uninteresting. *The tour guide's façade of enthusiasm could not hide his ennui.*

epitome (i·ˈpit·ŏ·mee) *n.* 1. something or someone that embodies a particular quality or characteristic, a representative example or a typical model 2. a brief summary or abstract. *Einstein is the epitome of true genius.*

ersatz (ĕr·ˈzăts) *adj.* artificial; being an imitation or substitute, especially one that is inferior. *Though most of the guests couldn't tell the difference, Waldo knew that the dish was made with ersatz truffles.*

façade (fă·ˈsahd) *n.* 1. the face or front of a building 2. an artificial or deceptive front, especially one intended to hide something unpleasant. *Antoine's stoicism is just a façade; he is really a deeply emotional person.*

gauche (gohsh) *adj.* 1. lacking social graces or polish; without tact 2. clumsy or awkward. *Attila is so gauche that it's embarrassing to be with him in public.*

gestalt (gĕ·shtălt) *n.* a configuration or pattern of elements so unified as a whole that it cannot be described merely as a sum of its parts. *One of the fundamental beliefs of gestalt therapy is that we exist in a web of relationships to other things, and that it is only possible to understand ourselves in the context of these relationships.*

hiatus (hī·ˈay·tŭs) *n.* a gap or opening; an interruption or break. *After he was laid off by the bank, Kobitu decided to take a long hiatus from the financial world and took a job as a middle school math teacher.*

hubris (ˈhyoo·bris) *n.* overbearing pride or presumption. *In the Greek tragedy* Oedipus Rex, *Oedipus's hubris leads to his downfall.*

imbroglio (im·ˈbrohl·yoh) *n.* a confused or difficult situation, usually involving a disagreement or misunderstanding. *In Shakespeare's comedies, there is often an imbroglio caused by a case of mistaken identity.*

incognito (in·ˈkog·nee·toh) *adj.* or *adv.* with one's identity concealed; in disguise or under an assumed character or identity. *The star was traveling incognito, hoping to find some measure of privacy on her vacation.*

insouciant (in·ˈsoo·si·ănt) *adj.* blithely unconcerned or carefree; nonchalant, indifferent. *Julian's insouciant attitude about his finances will get him in trouble someday.*

laissez-faire (les·ay·ˈfair) *adj.* hands-off policy; noninterference by the government in business and economic affairs. *Raheeb's laissez-faire management style is not only popular with our employees but also very successful—employee satisfaction is high and profits are up for the third quarter in a row.*

liaison (lee·ˈay·zon, ˈlee·ă·zon) *n.* 1. a channel or means of connection or communication between two groups; one who maintains such communication 2. a close relationship or link, especially one that is secretive or adulterous. *I have been elected to be the liaison between the union members and management.*

malaise (mă·ˈlayz) *n.* a feeling of illness or unease. *After several tests, Wella finally learned the cause of her malaise: She was allergic to her new Siamese cat.*

mélange (may·ˈlahnzh) *n.* a mixture or assortment. *The eclectic mélange of people at the party made for a scintillating evening.*

milieu (meel·ˈyuu) *n.* environment or setting. *The milieu at the writer's retreat is designed to inspire creativity.*

oeuvre (ˈuu·vrě) *n.* 1. a work of art 2. the total lifework of a writer, artist, composer, etc. *Constanta's latest oeuvre is an avant-garde symphony featuring a cow bell solo.*

par excellence (pahr ek·sě·lahns) *adj.* being the best or truest of its kind, quintessential; having the highest degree of excellence, beyond comparison. *Bob Hope was an entertainer par excellence.*

parvenu (ˈpahr·vě·noo) *n.* a person who has suddenly risen to a higher social or economic status but has not been socially accepted by others in that class; an upstart. *Ronnel was nice enough, of course, but because he was "new money" in an "old money" town, he was a parvenu who struggled to be accepted by his wealthy peers.*

SHORTCUT: FIND AN ENGLISH COUNTERPART

Most foreign words and phrases have an English synonym that you can use to help you remember meaning. For example, a synonym for *aficionado* is fan; a synonym for *milieu* is environment. These synonyms may not always completely capture the rich meaning of the word, but they can go a long way in helping you remember meaning.

quid pro quo (kwid·proh·ˈkwoh) *n.* a thing given in return for something; an equal exchange or substitution. *I won't agree to any deal that isn't quid pro quo—it must be a win-win arrangement.*

reconnoiter (ree·kŏ·ˈnoi·těr) *v.* to make a preliminary inspection or survey of, especially to gather military information or prepare for military operations. *My job was to reconnoiter the party and let my friends know if it was worth attending.*

rendezvous ('rahn·dĕ·voo) *n.* 1. a prearranged meeting at a certain time and place 2. a place where people meet, especially a popular gathering place; *v.* to bring or come together at a certain place, to meet at a rendezvous. *Clarissa and Ahmed planned a rendezvous in the park after lunch.*

savoir faire ('sav·wahr·'fair) *n.* knowledge of the right thing to do or say in a social situation; graceful tact. *Adele's savoir faire makes her the quintessential hostess.*

vignette (vin·'yet) *n.* a brief description or depiction, especially a short literary sketch or scene or ornamental sketch in a book. *The film is a series of interrelated vignettes rather than one continuous narrative.*

vis-à-vis (vee·ză·'vee) *adj.* 1. referring or directing attention to 2. face to face with or opposite to; *adv.* face to face. *After a few minutes of pandemonium, the lights came back on, and Suki suddenly found herself vis-à-vis with the man of her dreams.*

zeitgeist ('tsīt·gīst) *n.* the spirit of the times; the general intellectual and moral outlook or attitude characteristic of a particular generation or period of time. *The revolutionary zeitgeist of the sixties and seventies is in sharp contrast to the conservative zeitgeist of the fifties.*

TIPS AND STRATEGIES

Foreign words and phrases that have been adopted into the English language are likely to appear on standardized tests and occur regularly in newspaper articles, textbooks, and other day-to-day communications. Here are some specific tips and strategies to use as you add these words to your vocabulary and prepare for your exam.

- Use the context of the sentences provided with the definitions to help you understand these words and memorize their meanings.
- If you see a foreign word or phrase in a sentence, use the context to help you determine meaning. Look for clues to connotation as well as denotation.
- Remember to look for familiar prefixes, suffixes, and word roots. Although these words come from other languages, many prefixes and suffixes have the same meaning as in English, or the word may have English prefixes or suffixes added to foreign word bases. The Romance languages, including French, Spanish, and Italian, use many of the same Latin word roots as the English language. For example, *incognito*, an Italian word, uses the Latin root *gn/gno* meaning to know, while the French word *malaise* uses the prefix *mal-*, meaning bad, evil, wrong.

- Foreign words often do not have the standard English suffixes that help you identify parts of speech. As you memorize these words, be sure to note the part of speech of each word or phrase so you can use it correctly and identify its proper function in a sentence.
- Use all of the vocabulary knowledge you now have to eliminate incorrect answers on the exam. If a word has a prefix such as *in-* or *non-*, for example, you can often eliminate answers that do not express a negative.
- Solidify these words in your memory by teaching them to someone else.
- Pronounce these words each time you go over their meaning. The more you hear how they sound, the more familiar they will feel to you, and the easier it will be to remember them.
- Help yourself remember some of these words by finding a one-word English synonym whenever possible.
- Once again, use the power of mnemonic devices and associations to help you remember meaning.

 EXTRA HELP

If you want extra help with foreign words and phrases, you can find more review and practice in Lesson 8 of LearningExpress's *Vocabulary and Spelling Success in 20 Minutes a Day, 3rd edition.*

PRACTICE

For questions 1–25, identify the English synonym for each vocabulary word.

1. *milieu*
   a. quintessential
   b. actual
   c. arrogance
   d. environment
   e. upstart

2. *gauche*
   a. uncouth
   b. uneasy
   c. bored
   d. indifferent
   e. tactful

3. *mélange*
   a. meeting
   b. assortment
   c. disguise
   d. trite
   e. artificial

4. *parvenu*
   a. survey
   b. interruption
   c. upstart
   d. substitution
   e. cutting-edge

5. *insouciant*
   a. ill
   b. appropriate
   c. fan
   d. temporary
   e. nonchalant

6. *hiatus*
   a. opposition
   b. break
   c. awkward
   d. setting
   e. carefree

7. *par excellence*
   a. channel
   b. inspection
   c. depiction
   d. quintessential
   e. non-interference

8. *blasé*
   a. commonplace
   b. unconventional
   c. unconcerned
   d. factual
   e. opportune

9. *avant-garde*
   a. mixture
   b. incomparable
   c. prearranged
   d. unified
   e. innovative

10. *ennui*
   a. representative
   b. boredom
   c. abstraction
   d. polish
   e. opening

11. *malaise*
   a. lifework
   b. uneasiness
   c. indifference
   d. disagreement
   e. deception

12. *aficionado*
   a. devotee
   b. imitation
   c. attitude
   d. indulgence
   e. pride

13. *bourgeois*
   a. clumsy
   b. conceited
   c. truthful
   d. graceful
   e. middle-class

14. *epitome*
   a. sophistication
   b. gap
   c. exemplar
   d. pleasantry
   e. class

15. *reconnoiter*
   a. misunderstand
   b. describe
   c. moralize
   d. investigate
   e. link

16. *vignette*
   a. sketch
   b. presentation
   c. experiment
   d. pastime
   e. configuration

17. *laissez-faire*
   a. unique
   b. secretive
   c. hands-off
   d. self-satisfied
   e. artistic

18. *de facto*
   a. difficult
   b. actual
   c. intellectual
   d. concealed
   e. undivided

19. *rendezvous*
   a. inspection
   b. relationship
   c. conformity
   d. discontent
   e. meeting

20. *apropos*
   a. appropriate
   b. trite
   c. preliminary
   d. incorrect
   e. underestimated

21. *hubris*
   a. assumption
   b. exposure
   c. presumption
   d. communication
   e. source

22. *façade*
   a. pragmatism
   b. reference
   c. innovation
   d. pretense
   e. sophistication

23. *oeuvre*
   a. compilation
   b. mistreatment
   c. diversion
   d. appropriation
   e. summation

24. *incognito*
   a. temporary
   b. disguised
   c. inadequate
   d. misunderstood
   e. tedious

25. *savoir faire*
   a. government
   b. concern
   c. tact
   d. degree
   e. judgment

For questions 26–35, choose the vocabulary word whose meaning best matches the description.

26. when something is given in return for another thing of equal value
   a. apropos
   b. quid pro quo
   c. hubris
   d. liaison
   e. parvenu

27. a word to describe an inferior imitation or substitute
    a. mélange
    b. cliché
    c. par excellence
    d. oeuvre
    e. ersatz

28. confusion or chaos resulting from a misunderstanding
    a. mélange
    b. hiatus
    c. imbroglio
    d. zeitgeist
    e. façade

29. a word to describe an account set up specifically for college savings
    a. ad hoc
    b. insouciant
    c. bourgeois
    d. avant-garde
    e. incognito

30. the first time an actor performs on Broadway
    a. milieu
    b. rendezvous
    c. vignette
    d. debut
    e. epitome

31. a phrase used to refer or direct attention to
    a. avant-garde
    b. de facto
    c. quid pro quo
    d. vis-à-vis
    e. ad hoc

32. the general spirit or mood of a particular era
    a. ennui
    b. zeitgeist
    c. parvenu
    d. hiatus
    e. milieu

33. a saying that is overused, hackneyed
   a. savoir faire
   b. aficionado
   c. hubris
   d. oeuvre
   e. cliché

34. the relationship between a parasite and its host, for example, or the elements of an ecosystem
   a. gestalt
   b. vignette
   c. malaise
   d. blasé
   e. gauche

35. the person who maintains communication between two groups
   a. aficionado
   b. epitome
   c. liaison
   d. rendezvous
   e. laissez-faire

ANSWERS

1. d. *Milieu* means environment or setting.

2. a. *Gauche* means (1) lacking social graces or polish; without tact; (2) clumsy or awkward.

3. b. A *mélange* is a mixture or assortment.

4. c. A *parvenu* is a person who has suddenly risen to a higher social or economic status but has not been socially accepted by others in that class; an upstart.

5. e. *Insouciant* means blithely unconcerned or carefree; nonchalant, indifferent.

6. b. A *hiatus* is a gap or opening; an interruption or break.

7. d. *Par excellence* means being the best or truest of its kind, quintessential; having the highest degree of excellence, beyond comparison.

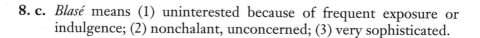
8. c. *Blasé* means (1) uninterested because of frequent exposure or indulgence; (2) nonchalant, unconcerned; (3) very sophisticated.

9. e. *Avant-garde* means using or favoring an ultramodern or experimental style; innovative, cutting edge, especially in arts or literature.

10. b. *Ennui* means boredom and listlessness resulting from something tedious or uninteresting.

11. b. *Malaise* is a feeling of illness or unease.

12. a. An *aficionado* is a fan or devotee, especially of a sport or pastime.

13. e. *Bourgeois* means typical of the middle class; conforming to the standards and conventions of the middle class; hence also, commonplace, conservative, or materialistic.

14. c. *Epitome* means (1) something or someone that embodies a particular quality or characteristic, a representative example or a typical model; (2) a brief summary or abstract.

15. d. To *reconnoiter* means to make a preliminary inspection or survey of, especially to gather military information or prepare for military operations.

16. a. A *vignette* is a brief description or depiction, especially a short literary sketch or scene or ornamental sketch in a book.

17. c. *Laissez-faire* means hands-off policy; noninterference by the government in business and economic affairs.

18. b. *De facto* means in reality or fact; actual.

19. e. The noun *rendezvous* means (1) a prearranged meeting at a certain time and place; (2) a place where people meet, especially a popular gathering place. The verb *rendezvous* means to bring or come together at a certain place, to meet at a rendezvous.

20. a. *Apropos* means appropriate to the situation; suitable to what is being said or done. As an adverb, it also means (1) by the way, incidentally; (2) at an appropriate or opportune time.

21. c. *Hubris* means overbearing pride or presumption.

22. d. A *façade* is (1) the face or front of a building; (2) an artificial or deceptive front, especially one intended to hide something unpleasant.

23. a. An *oeuvre* is (1) a work of art; (2) the total lifework of a writer, artist, composer, etc.; hence, a compilation.

24. b. *Incognito* means with one's identity concealed; in disguise or under an assumed character or identity.

25. c. *Savoir faire* is knowledge of the right thing to do or say in a social situation; graceful tact.

26. b. *Quid pro quo* means a thing given in return for something; an equal exchange or substitution.

27. e. *Ersatz* means artificial; being an imitation or substitute, especially one that is inferior.

28. c. An *imbroglio* is a confused or difficult situation, usually involving a disagreement or misunderstanding.

29. a. *Ad hoc* means for a specific, often temporary purpose; for this case only.

30. d. A *debut* is a first appearance in or presentation to the public.

31. d. *Vis-à-vis* means (1) referring or directing attention to; (2) face to face with or opposite to.

32. b. *Zeitgeist* is the spirit of the times; the general intellectual and moral outlook or attitude characteristic of a particular generation or period of time.

33. e. A *cliché* is a trite or overused expression or idea.

34. a. *Gestalt* is a configuration or pattern of elements so unified as a whole that it cannot be described merely as a sum of its parts.

35. c. *Liaison* means (1) a channel or means of connection or communication between two groups; one who maintains such communication; (2) a close relationship or link, especially one that is secretive or adulterous.

10

$5 Words

What does *hermetic* mean? What is a *juggernaut*? What does it mean to be *obsequious*? In this final chapter, you will learn these and many more "$5" words to help you develop a more sophisticated vocabulary and ace the most difficult questions on your exam. Before you begin learning and reviewing versatile verbs, take a few minutes to take this ten-question *Benchmark Quiz*. These questions are similar to the type of questions that you will find on important tests. When you are finished, check the answer key carefully to assess your results. Your Benchmark Quiz analysis will help you determine how much time you need to spend on reviewing the $5 words you need to learn in order to increase your vocabulary power.

BENCHMARK QUIZ

Select the answer that provides the meaning of the vocabulary word.

1. *clandestine*
   a. recklessly endangering others
   b. conducted in secrecy
   c. to underestimate the value of
   d. an attempted but failed revolution
   e. unwilling to compromise

2. *inculcate*
   a. to undermine
   b. without fail, certain
   c. to convert
   d. to indoctrinate
   e. an extended period of mourning

3. *archaic*
   a. uncontrollable
   b. insincere
   c. ancient
   d. insight
   e. to worry

4. *succor*
   a. assistance in a time of distress
   b. to be addicted to sweets
   c. to feel obligated to others
   d. daring, bold
   e. an inability to trust others

5. *evanescent*
   a. childlike
   b. to recommend highly
   c. divided into equal parts
   d. vanishing like vapor
   e. a brief summary or explanation

6. *laconic*
   a. overpriced
   b. imperceptible
   c. terse
   d. to teem
   e. one who rebels against authority

7. *punctilious*
   a. without regard for rules or regulations
   b. very precise and attentive to detail
   c. to unknowingly mislead others
   d. a minor mistake
   e. very emotional writing

8. *desultory*
   a. obsessed with beauty
   b. to reveal by degrees
   c. unconventional
   d. aimless or haphazard
   e. a place to store grain

9. *pecuniary*
   a. having to do with money
   b. related to a previous occurrence
   c. one who demands justice
   d. to absorb slowly
   e. so small as to be immeasurable

10. *oscillate*
   a. to relinquish
   b. only once
   c. heavily armed
   d. to deny
   e. to waver

BENCHMARK QUIZ SOLUTIONS

How did you do on identifying $5 words? Check your answers here, and then analyze the results to figure out your plan of attack for mastering this topic.

▶ Answers

1. b. *Clandestine* means conducted in secrecy; kept or done in private, often in order to conceal an illicit or improper purpose.

2. d. To *inculcate* means to teach and impress by frequent instruction or repetition; to indoctrinate, instill.

3. c. *Archaic* means belonging to former or ancient times; characteristic of the past.

4. a. *Succor* means (1) *n.* assistance or relief in time of difficulty or distress; (2) *v.* to provide assistance or relief in time of difficulty or distress.

5. d. *Evanescent* means vanishing or tending to vanish like vapor; transitory, fleeting.

6. c. *Laconic* means brief and to the point; succinct, terse, concise.

7. b. *Punctilious* means extremely attentive to detail; very meticulous and precise.

8. d. *Desultory* means aimless, haphazard; moving from one subject to another without logical connection.

9. a. *Pecuniary* means of, relating to, or involving money.

10. e. To *oscillate* means (1) to swing back and forth or side to side in a steady, uninterrupted rhythm; (2) to waver, as between two conflicting options or opinions; vacillate.

BENCHMARK QUIZ RESULTS

If you answered 8–10 questions correctly, well done! You are already familiar with many of these advanced vocabulary words. Give the lesson a quick review and do the practice exercise. If your score on the practice test is equally high, congratulations—you have completed the last chapter and have added over 350 words to your vocabulary!

If you answered 4–7 questions correctly, you already know some of these advanced vocabulary words, but you need more of these commonly tested $5 words in your permanent vocabulary. Be sure to set aside some time to carefully review the vocabulary words listed in this chapter.

If you answered 1–3 questions correctly, you may have a strong basic vocabulary, but you need to add some more advanced vocabulary words to your word base. Study the lesson that follows carefully, and do the practice quiz on a separate sheet of paper so that you can do the exercise several times if necessary.

JUST IN TIME LESSON—$5 WORDS

Abstemious, desultory, lugubrious . . . Some words just seem like they were made for vocabulary exams! The "$5 words" in this chapter represent the kind of advanced vocabulary terms that often appear on more difficult vocabulary tests. They are words that most people are not very familiar with. For example, even if you are one of the most meticulous people you know, you may never have been called *punctilious*, and you may never have heard something from the distant past characterized as *archaic*. But that doesn't mean these words are not important or useful or even that they are not quite common in some circles. Though they may appear less often in our every day communications than the words in previous chapters, they do appear regularly in more sophisticated texts, such as college-level textbooks and professional essays, and yes, they do often appear on vocabulary exams as a way to measure the full extent of your vocabulary.

Adding $5 words like these to your vocabulary offers numerous benefits. First, you will understand more of what you read and hear. Second, you will be able to express yourself more effectively. Third, during interviews and other important occasions, you will often impress others with your sophisticated vocabulary. And fourth, knowing a lot of $5 words can help you take your exam score to a new level.

As with the words you learned in previous lessons, these advanced vocabulary words will help you pinpoint meaning and express the precise connotation you wish to convey. For example, *punctilious* is a synonym of *meticulous* (Chapter 7), but it expresses an even stronger, almost obsessive attention to detail:

> *meticulous:* extremely careful and precise; paying great attention to detail
> *punctilious:* extremely attentive to detail, very meticulous and precise

A *punctilious* person, then, is not just meticulous, but *very* meticulous. By knowing this distinction, you can choose the word that expresses the appropriate degree.

Indeed, notice how many of these vocabulary words build on your existing word base. Several of them have words from previous chapters in their definitions or are synonymous with words from other lessons. *Ascetic*, for example, means *austere*, a word from Chapter 7; *laconic* means *terse* (Chapter 2) or *succinct* (Chapter 7). *Oscillate* is a synonym of *vacillate* (Chapter 8), and *vituperate* means to *censure* (Chapter 6) severely or *rebuke* (Chapter 8) harshly. An *obsequious* person is excessively *servile* (Chapter 7) while *clandestine* is a synonym of *surreptitious* (Chapter 7).

RULE BOOK: ALL SYNONYMS ARE NOT CREATED EQUAL

Although some synonyms are interchangeable, it is important to remember that most words have their own unique connotation. So while exam questions will often ask you to identify synonyms such as *laconic, terse*, and *succinct*, when it comes to your own communications, you should choose your words carefully. *Terse*, for example, has the most positive connotation of these three words, suggesting brevity with a sense of polish or elegance. *Succinct* is more neutral, conveying a sense of compactness or tightness in how an idea has been expressed. *Laconic*, on the other hand, conveys the same basic idea but with the suggestion of brusqueness or abruptness. Thus, although these words are effectively synonymous, each word carries its own specific connotation and leaves a slightly different impression.

Other words in this lesson have meanings that are unlike any other word in this book and are often used in specific contexts. An *epiphany*, for example, is a sudden, intuitive realization of the essence or meaning of something, a perceptive revelation; a manifestation of the divine. To *gerrymander*, meanwhile, means to divide an area into voting districts so as to give one party an unfair advantage.

The 35 upper-level vocabulary words in this chapter will help you develop a more sophisticated vocabulary and feel more confident when you see $5 words on your exam. There are nouns, verbs, and adjectives—many of which use common suffix endings for their part of speech. Once more, each definition in the list below includes a sample sentence to show how the word is used in context. Learn these words well to boost your test score, to understand more of what you read and hear, and to more accurately express yourself in your day-to-day communications.

WORD LIST

abstemious (ab·'stee·mi·ŭs) *adj.* 1. using or consuming sparingly; used with temperance or moderation 2. eating and drinking in moderation; sparing in the indulgence of appetites or passions. *After Vadeem gained 30 pounds, he decided he needed a more abstemious diet.*

acumen (ă·'kyoo·měn) *n.* quickness, keenness, and accuracy of perception, judgment, or insight. *With Jonelle's acumen, she would make an excellent trial lawyer.*

archaic (ahr·'kay·ik) *adj.* belonging to former or ancient times; characteristic of the past. *The archaic language of Chaucer's tales makes them difficult for many students to understand.*

ascetic (ă·'set·ik) *adj.* practicing self-denial, not allowing oneself pleasures or luxuries; austere. *Eli was attracted to the peaceful, spiritual life of the monks, but he knew he could not handle such an ascetic lifestyle.*

bowdlerize ('bohd·lĕ·rīz) *v.* to edit by omitting or modifying parts that may be considered offensive; censor. *To make their collection of fairy tales suitable for children, the Brothers Grimm had to bowdlerize the folk tales they had collected, for many of the original tales included graphic language.*

chimera (ki·'meer·ă) *n.* 1. (in Greek mythology) a fire-breathing she-monster with a lion's head, a goat's body, and a serpent's tail 2. a vain or incongruous fancy; a (monstrous) product of the imagination, illusion. *Seduced by the chimera of immortality, Victor Frankenstein created a monster that ended up destroying him and everyone he loved.*

clandestine (klan·'des·tin) *adj.* conducted in secrecy; kept or done in private, often in order to conceal an illicit or improper purpose. *The private investigator followed Raul to a clandestine rendezvous with a woman in sunglasses and a trench coat.*

coeval (koh·'ee·văl) *adj.* of the same time period, contemporary. *The poet Ben Johnson was a coeval of Shakespeare.*

desultory ('des·ŭl·tohr·ee) *adj.* aimless, haphazard; moving from one subject to another without logical connection. *Ichabod's desultory ramblings worsened as his disease progressed.*

epiphany (i·'pif·ă·nee) *n.* 1. a sudden, intuitive realization of the essence or meaning of something, a perceptive revelation 2. a manifestation of the divine *As I listened to Professor Lane's lecture, I had a sudden epiphany that I was in the wrong major.*

evanescent (ev·ă·'nes·ĕnt) *adj.* vanishing or tending to vanish like vapor; transitory, fleeting. *The subject of the poem is the evanescent nature of young love.*

SHORTCUT: MNEMONICS ONCE MORE

Combine your other study strategies such as flashcards with mnemonic devices that will help you remember meaning. For example, you can remember the meaning of *gerrymander* with a sentence such as *Gerry was unfairly elected through gerrymandering.* Or, you can remember *hermetic* by associating it with a hermit, who is likely to have limited outside influences.

fallacy ('fal·ă·see) *n.* a false notion or misconception resulting from incorrect or illogical reasoning 2. that which is deceptive or has a false appearance; something that misleads, deception. *The "slippery slope" fallacy argues that once X happens, Y and Z will automatically follow.*

gerrymander ('jer·i·man·dĕr) *v.* to divide an area into voting districts so as to give one party an unfair advantage *n.* the act of gerrymandering. *The election was rigged by gerrymandering that gave unfair advantage to the incumbent.*

hegemony (hi·'jem·ŏ·nee) *n.* predominant influence or leadership, especially of one government over others. *The hegemony of his country borders on imperialism.*

hermetic (hur·'met·ik) *adj.* 1. having an airtight closure 2. protected from outside influences. *In the hermetic world of the remote mountain convent, the nuns did not even know that their country was on the brink of war.*

impugn (im·'pyoon) *v.* to attack as false or questionable; to contradict or call into question. *The editorial impugned the senator's reelection platform and set the tone for the upcoming debate.*

inculcate (in·'kul·kayt) *v.* to teach and impress by frequent instruction or repetition; to indoctrinate, instill. *My parents worked hard to inculcate in me a deep sense of responsibility to others.*

jejune (ji·'joon) *adj.* lacking substance, meager; hence: (a) lacking in interest or significance; insipid or dull, (b) lacking in maturity, childish, (c) lacking nutritional value. *The movie's trite and overly-contrived plot make it a jejune sequel to what was a powerful and novel film.*

CHEAT SHEET: WATCH FOR SHAPE-SHIFTERS

By mastering the 350+ words in this book, you are really expanding your vocabulary by closer to 500 words. That's because hundreds more words can be formed by adding or changing prefixes and/or suffixes on the words in these chapters. The adjective *evanescent*, for example, can become the noun *evanescence:*

> *evanescent:* vanishing or tending to vanish like vapor; transitory, fleeting
> *evanescence:* the state of being evanescent

Likewise, the noun *hegemony* can become the adjective *hegemonic:*

> *hegemony:* predominant influence or leadership, especially of one government over others
> *hegemonic:* leading or ruling; controlling, predominant

On your exam, you may see the words in the same form that you have memorized from this book. But, do be on the lookout for alternate forms, and use your knowledge of prefixes and suffixes to determine meaning.

juggernaut ('jug·ĕr·nawt) *n.* a massive, overwhelmingly powerful and unstoppable force that seems to crush everything in its path. *A shroud of fear covered Eastern Europe as the juggernaut of Communism spread from nation to nation.*

laconic (lă·ˈkon·ik) *adj.* brief and to the point; succinct, terse, concise, often to the point of being curt or brusque. *Zse's laconic reply made it clear that he did not want to discuss the matter any further.*

lugubrious (luu·ˈgoo·bri·ŭs) *adj.* excessively dismal or mournful, often exaggeratedly or ridiculously so. *Irina's lugubrious tears made me believe that her sadness was just a façade.*

machination (mak·ĭ·ˈnay·shŏn) *n.* 1. the act of plotting or devising 2. a crafty or cunning scheme devised to achieve a sinister end. *Macbeth's machinations failed to bring him the glory he coveted and brought him only tragedy instead.*

SHORT CUT: HAPPY COUPLES

As you have already seen, many of these $5 words have synonyms elsewhere in this book. Pair up the words in this chapter with other vocabulary words to help you remember meaning. They can be synonym or antonym pairs (e.g., *bowdlerize* and *censor*) or just useful associations, such as *inculcate* and *proselytize*.

myriad (ˈmir·i·ăd) *adj.* too numerous to be counted; innumerable; *n.* an indefinitely large number; an immense number, vast amount. *To the refugees from Somalia, the myriad choices in the American supermarket were overwhelming.*

obsequious (ŏb·ˈsee·kwi·ŭs) *adj.* excessively or ingratiatingly compliant or submissive; attentive in a servile or ingratiating manner, fawning. *The obsequious manner of the butler made it clear that he resented his position.*

oscillate (ˈos·ĭ·layt) *v.* 1. to swing back and forth or side to side in a steady, uninterrupted rhythm 2. to waver, as between two conflicting options or opinions; vacillate. *The rhythm of the oscillating fan put the baby to sleep.*

pecuniary (pi·ˈkyoo·ni·er·ee) *adj.* of, relating to, or involving money. *Rosen was relieved to learn that his penalty would be pecuniary only and that he would not have to spend any time in jail.*

proselytize (ˈpros·ĕ·li·tīz) *v.* to convert or seek to convert someone to another religion, belief, doctrine or cause. *After a few minutes, it became clear to Hannah that the purpose of the meeting was really to proselytize as many attendees as possible.*

propinquity (proh·ˈping·kwi·tee) *n.* 1. proximity, nearness 2. affinity, similarity in nature. *The propinquity of these two elements make them difficult to tell apart.*

punctilious (pungk·ˈtil·i·ŭs) *adj.* extremely attentive to detail, very meticulous and precise. *One of the reasons he excels as an editor is because he is so punctilious.*

seditious (si·'dish·ŭs) *adj.* arousing to insurrection or rebellion; engaging in or promoting sedition (conduct or language which incites resistance or opposition to lawful authority). *Toby's seditious behavior nearly started a riot at the town meeting.*

CHEAT SHEET: BEGINNINGS, MIDDLES, AND ENDS

As you review these words, don't forget about word parts. Use prefixes, suffixes, and word roots to help you better understand and remember the words in this lesson.

succor ('suk·ŏr) *n.* assistance or relief in time of difficulty or distress; *v.* to provide assistance or relief in time of difficulty or distress. *The Red Cross and other relief organizations provide succor to the needy during natural disasters.*

surfeit ('sur·fit) *v.* to feed or fill to excess, satiety, or disgust; overindulge; *n.* 1. an excessive amount or overabundance; glut 2. the state of being or eating until excessively full. *In many third-world countries, the leaders and a select few enjoy a surfeit of wealth while most of the population lives in squalor.*

sycophant ('sik·ŏ·fănt) *n.* a person who tries to win the favor of influential or powerful people through flattery; a fawning parasite. *Omar realized that one of the drawbacks of his celebrity was that he would always be surrounded by sycophants.*

unctuous ('ungk·choo·ŭs) *adj.* 1. unpleasantly and excessively or insincerely earnest or ingratiating 2. containing or having the quality of oil or ointment; greasy, slippery, suave. *I left without test driving the car because the salesperson was so unctuous that I couldn't trust him.*

vituperate (vī·'too·pĕ·rayt) *v.* to criticize or rebuke harshly or abusively; to censure severely, berate. *After being vituperated by her boss for something that wasn't even her fault, Jin handed in her letter of resignation.*

TIPS AND STRATEGIES

Though $5 words may seem intimidating, you can tackle them with the same strategies you have been using all throughout this book. Here are some specific tips and strategies to use as you countdown to your exam.

- Remember all of the vocabulary tools you already have at your disposal. Use context (if available), prefixes and suffixes, and word roots to help you determine meaning; use the process of elimination to help narrow down your answer choices.
- Read each definition and sample sentence carefully to fully understand each word and its connotation.

- Remember the power of mnemonic devices to help you memorize new words. Create memorable rhymes, images, or sentences that will help you recall meaning.
- Make your study time doubly productive by matching the words in this lesson with words from other chapters. You can group together words with the same or opposite meanings or words that share a particular association.
- Pay attention to connotation and degree. *Machination*, for example, is not just a scheme; it's a *crafty* scheme, one that suggests an evil purpose.
- Review, review, review. In whatever time you have left before your exam, review the words in this book as much as you can. The more you review them, the more quickly they will become part of your permanent vocabulary and the more comfortable you will feel using them in your conversations and writing. Make note of the chapters with which you had the most difficulty and set aside extra time for those words. Come back to these chapters after your exam, too. You will not only have improved your vocabulary just in time—you will have a rich vocabulary for all time.

PRACTICE

For questions 1–20, choose the vocabulary word that matches the definition.

1. a sudden, intuitive realization of the essence or meaning of something
   a. propinquity
   b. epiphany
   c. sycophant
   d. machination
   e. acumen

2. of, relating to, or involving money
   a. lugubrious
   b. archaic
   c. coeval
   d. pecuniary
   e. unctuous

3. used or consumed sparingly or in moderation
   a. abstemious
   b. hermetic
   c. ascetic
   d. evanescent
   e. laconic

4. a crafty or cunning scheme with a sinister purpose
   a. juggernaut
   b. fallacy
   c. gerrymander
   d. hegemony
   e. machination

5. excessively dismal or mournful
   a. obsequious
   b. seditious
   c. lugubrious
   d. jejune
   e. clandestine

6. to seek to convert someone to another religion, belief, or cause
   a. bowdlerize
   b. proselytize
   c. oscillate
   d. inculcate
   e. vituperate

7. to provide assistance or relief in time of difficulty
   a. succor
   b. impugn
   c. gerrymander
   d. surfeit
   e. inculcate

8. someone who tries to win the favor of the influential or powerful through flattery
   a. chimera
   b. coeval
   c. hermetic
   d. sycophant
   e. juggernaut

9. belonging to former or ancient times
   a. desultory
   b. archaic
   c. myriad
   d. pecuniary
   e. seditious

10. protected from outside influences
    a. jejune
    b. unctuous
    c. lugubrious
    d. hermetic
    e. laconic

11. the predominant influence or leadership, especially of one government over others
    a. hegemony
    b. propinquity
    c. succor
    d. fallacy
    e. epiphany

12. quickness, keenness, and accuracy of perception or judgment
    a. myriad
    b. machinations
    c. acumen
    d. propinquity
    e. sycophant

13. lacking substance, meager; insipid, childish, or of little nutritional value
    a. abstemious
    b. jejune
    c. seditious
    d. punctilious
    e. obsequious

14. a massive, overwhelmingly powerful and unstoppable force that seems to crush everything in its path
    a. epiphany
    b. surfeit
    c. hegemony
    d. juggernaut
    e. fallacy

15. arousing to insurrection or rebellion
    a. desultory
    b. lugubrious
    c. clandestine
    d. pecuniary
    e. seditious

16. a false notion or misconception resulting from incorrect or illogical reasoning
    a. fallacy
    b. succor
    c. sycophant
    d. chimera
    e. acumen

17. unpleasantly and excessively or insincerely ingratiating
    a. unctuous
    b. coeval
    c. abstemious
    d. evanescent
    e. jejune

18. to divide an area into voting districts so as to give one party an unfair advantage
    a. bowdlerize
    b. impugn
    c. inculcate
    d. oscillate
    e. gerrymander

19. aimless, haphazard; moving form one subject to another without logical connection
    a. laconic
    b. archaic
    c. desultory
    d. hermetic
    e. clandestine

20. to attack as false or questionable; to contradict or call into question
    a. proselytize
    b. succor
    c. vituperate
    d. impugn
    e. surfeit

For questions 21–35, choose the best synonym for the vocabulary word.

21. chimera
   a. deception
   b. illusion
   c. denial
   d. fable
   e. closure

22. propinquity
   a. affinity
   b. assistance
   c. abuse
   d. appearance
   e. resistance

23. inculcate
   a. destabilize
   b. legitimize
   c. contradict
   d. instill
   e. modify

24. myriad
   a. pensive
   b. insignificant
   c. innumerable
   d. eloquent
   e. uncompromising

25. vituperate
   a. promote
   b. berate
   c. flatter
   d. disdain
   e. relinquish

26. punctilious
   a. timely
   b. daunting
   c. erratic
   d. meticulous
   e. trite

27. evanescent
   a. transitory
   b. massive
   c. erratic
   d. miscellaneous
   e. futile

28. surfeit
   a. dissension
   b. pleasantry
   c. overabundance
   d. accommodation
   e. proximity

29. ascetic
   a. incessant
   b. austere
   c. surreptitious
   d. quiescent
   e. timid

30. coeval
   a. exaggerated
   b. cooperative
   c. malicious
   d. contemporary
   e. courteous

31. oscillate
   a. appease
   b. garner
   c. winnow
   d. corroborate
   e. vacillate

32. laconic
   a. gauche
   b. stoic
   c. succinct
   d. impervious
   e. loquacious

33. clandestine
   a. surreptitious
   b. noxious
   c. virulent
   d. pervasive
   e. amiable

34. bowdlerize
   a. placate
   b. censor
   c. abhor
   d. rectify
   e. surmise

35. obsequious
   a. ensconced
   b. meandering
   c. blasé
   d. fawning
   e. mundane

ANSWERS

1. b. An *epiphany* is (1) a sudden, intuitive realization of the essence or meaning of something, a perceptive revelation; (2) a manifestation of the divine.

2. d. *Pecuniary* means of, relating to, or involving money.

3. a. *Abstemious* means (1) using or consuming sparingly; used with temperance or moderation; (2) eating and drinking in moderation; sparing in the indulgence of appetites or passions.

4. e. *Machination* is (1) the act of plotting or devising; (2) a crafty or cunning scheme devised to achieve a sinister end.

5. c. *Lugubrious* means excessively dismal or mournful, often exaggeratedly or ridiculously so.

6. b. To *proselytize* means to convert or seek to convert someone to another religion, belief, doctrine or cause.

7. a. The noun *succor* means assistance or relief in time of difficulty or distress; the verb form means to provide assistance or relief in time of difficulty or distress.

8. d. A *sycophant* is a person who tries to win the favor of influential or powerful people through flattery; a fawning parasite.

9. b. *Archaic* means belonging to former or ancient times; characteristic of the past.

10. d. *Hermetic* means (1) having an airtight closure; (2) protected from outside influences.

11. a. *Hegemony* is predominant influence or leadership, especially of one government over others.

12. c. *Acumen* means quickness, keenness, and accuracy of perception, judgment, or insight.

13. b. *Jejune* means lacking substance, meager; hence: (a) lacking in interest or significance; insipid or dull (b) lacking in maturity, childish (c) lacking nutritional value.

14. d. A *juggernaut* is a massive, overwhelmingly powerful and unstoppable force that seems to crush everything in its path.

15. e. *Seditious* means arousing to insurrection or rebellion; engaging in or promoting sedition (conduct or language which incites resistance or opposition to lawful authority).

16. a. A *fallacy* is (1) a false notion or misconception resulting from incorrect or illogical reasoning; (2) that which is deceptive or has a false appearance; something that misleads, deception.

17. a. *Unctuous* means (1) unpleasantly and excessively or insincerely earnest or ingratiating; (2) containing or having the quality of oil or ointment; greasy, slippery, suave.

18. e. To *gerrymander* means to divide an area into voting districts so as to give one party an unfair advantage; as a noun, the act of gerrymandering.

19. c. *Desultory* means aimless, haphazard; moving from one subject to another without logical connection.

20. d. To *impugn* means to attack as false or questionable; to contradict or call into question.

21. b. A *chimera* is (1) (in Greek mythology) a fire-breathing she-monster with a lion's head, a goat's body, and a serpent's tail; (2) a vain or incongruous fancy; a (monstrous) product of the imagination, illusion.

22. a. *Propinquity* means (1) proximity, nearness; (2) affinity, similarity in nature.

23. d. To *inculcate* is to teach and impress by frequent instruction or repetition; to indoctrinate, instill.

24. c. The adjective *myriad* means too numerous to be counted; innumerable. As a noun it means an indefinitely large number; an immense number, vast amount.

25. b. To *vituperate* means to criticize or rebuke harshly or abusively; to censure severely, berate.

26. d. *Punctilious* means extremely attentive to detail, very meticulous and precise.

27. a. *Evanescent* means vanishing or tending to vanish like vapor; transitory, fleeting.

28. c. The verb *surfeit* means to feed or fill to excess, satiety, or disgust; overindulge. As a noun it means (1) an excessive amount or overabundance, glut; (2) the state of being or eating until excessively full.

29. b. *Ascetic* means practicing self-denial, not allowing oneself pleasures or luxuries; austere.

30. d. *Coeval* means of the same time period, contemporary.

31. e. To *oscillate* means (1) to swing back and forth or side to side in a steady, uninterrupted rhythm; (2) to waver, as between two conflicting options or opinions; vacillate.

32. c. *Laconic* means brief and to the point; succinct, terse, concise, often to the point of being curt or brusque.

33. a. *Clandestine* means conducted in secrecy; kept or done in private, often in order to conceal an illicit or improper purpose.

34. b. To *bowdlerize* means to edit by omitting or modifying parts that may be considered offensive; censor.

35. d. *Obsequious* means excessively or ingratiatingly compliant or submissive; attentive or servile in an ingratiating manner, fawning.

APPENDIX A

Prefixes, Suffixes, and Word Roots

PREFIXES

The following table lists the most common English language prefixes, their meanings, and several examples of words with each prefix. Whenever possible, the examples include both common words that are already part of your everyday vocabulary *and* words from the lessons in this book.

PREFIX	MEANING	EXAMPLES
a-, an-	not, without	atypical, anarchy, amorphous
ab-, abs-	from, away, off	abnormal, abduct, abscond
ante-	prior to, in front of, before	antedate, antecedent, antebellum
ant-, anti-	opposite, opposing, against	antidote, antagonist, antipathy
bi-	two, twice	bisect, bilateral, bicameral
circum-	around, about, on all sides	circumference, circumnavigate, circumspect
co-, com-, con-	with, together, jointly cooperate,	community, consensus
contra-	against, contrary, contrasting	contradict, contraindication
counter-	contrary, opposite or opposing; complementary	counterclockwise, countermeasure, counterpart
de-	do the opposite or reverse of; remove from, reduce	deactivate, dethrone, detract

PREFIX	MEANING	EXAMPLES
dis-	away from, apart, reversal, not	disperse, dismiss, disinterested
duo-	two	duo, duet, duality
ex-	out, out of, away from	expel, exclaim, exorbitant
in- (*also* il-, im-, ir-)	in, into, within	induct, impart, inculcate
in- (*also* il-, im-, ir-)	not	invariable, incessant, illicit, inept, impervious
inter-	between, among, within	intervene, interact, intermittent
intra-	within, during	intramural, intravenous
intro-	in, into, within	introvert, introduction
mal-	bad, abnormal, evil, wrong	malfunction, malpractice, malign
mis-	bad, wrong, ill; opposite; lack of	misspell, miscreant, misanthrope
mono-	one, single, alone	monologue, monogamy, monocle
multi-	many, multiple	multiple, multimillionaire, multifarious
neo-	new, recent, a new form of	neologism, neonatal, neophyte
non-	not	nonconformist, nonentity, nonchalant
over-	exceeding, surpassing, excessive	overabundance, overstimulate
poly-	many, much	polyester, polytechnic, polyglot
post-	after, subsequent, later (than), behind	postpone, postpartum, postoperative
pre-	before	precaution, precede, presage
pro-	(a) earlier, before, prior to; in front of (b) for, supporting, in behalf of (c) forward, projecting	proceed, proclivity, profess
pseudo-	false, fake	pseudonym, pseudoscience
re-	back, again	recall, reconcile, rescind
semi-	half, partly, incomplete	semiannual, semiconscious
sub-	under, beneath, below	subconscious, subdue, subjugate
super-	above, over, exceeding	superhero, superficial, supercilious
trans-	across, beyond, through	transmit, translate, translucent
tri-	three, thrice	triangle, tricycle, triumvirate
un-	not	unable, uninterested, unorthodox
uni-	one	unite, uniform, unilateral

SUFFIXES

The following table lists the most common English language suffixes, their meanings, and several examples of words with each suffix. Whenever possible, the examples include both common words that are already part of your everyday vocabulary *and* words from the lessons in this book.

NOUN ENDINGS

SUFFIX	MEANING	EXAMPLES
-age	(a) action or process (b) house or place of (c) state, rank	drainage, orphanage, marriage
-al	action or process	rehearsal, disposal, reversal
-an, -ian	of or relating to; a person specializing in	guardian, pediatrician, historian
-ance, -ence	action or process; state of	adolescence, benevolence, renaissance
-ancy, -ency	quality or state	agency, vacancy, latency
-ant, -ent	one that performs, promotes, or causes an action; being in a specified state or condition	disinfectant, dissident, miscreant
-ary	thing belonging to or connected with	adversary, dignitary, library
-cide	killer, killing	suicide, pesticide, homicide
-cy	action or practice; state or quality of	democracy, legitimacy, supremacy
-er, -or	one that is, does, or performs	builder, foreigner, sensor
-ion, -tion	act or process; state or condition	attraction, persecution, denunciation
-ism	act, practice, or process; state or doctrine of	criticism, anachronism, imperialism
-ist	one who (performs, makes, produces, believes, etc.)	anarchist, feminist, imperialist
-ity	quality, state, or degree	clarity, amity, veracity
-ment	action or process; result, object, means, or agent of an action or process	entertainment, embankment, amazement
-ness	state, condition, quality or degree	happiness, readiness, goodness
-ology	doctrine, theory, or science; oral or written expression	biology, theology, eulogy
-or	condition, activity	candor, valor, succor
-sis	process or action	diagnosis, dialysis, metamorphosis
-ure	act or process; office or function	exposure, legislature, censure
-y	state, condition, quality; activity or place of business	laundry, empathy, anarchy

ADJECTIVE ENDINGS

SUFFIX	MEANING	EXAMPLES
-able, -ible	capable or worthy of; tending or liable to	flammable, culpable, inscrutable
-al, -ial, -ical	having the quality of; of, relating to, or characterized by	educational, peripheral, ephemeral
-an, -ian	one who is or does; related to, characteristic of	human, American, agrarian
-ant, -ent	performing (a specific action) or being (in a specified condition)	important, incessant, preeminent
-ful	full of; having the qualities of; tending or liable to	helpful, peaceful, wistful
-ic	pertaining or relating to; having the quality of	fantastic, chronic, archaic
-ile	tending to or capable of	fragile, futile, servile
-ish	having the quality of	Swedish, bookish, squeamish
-ive	performing or tending towards (an action); having the nature of	sensitive, cooperative, pensive
-less	without, lacking; unable to act or be acted on (in a specified way)	endless, fearless, listless
-ous, -ose,	full of, having the qualities of, relating to	adventurous, glorious, egregious
-y	characterized by, full of; tending or inclined to	sleepy, cursory, desultory

VERB ENDINGS

SUFFIX	MEANING	EXAMPLES
-ate	to make, to cause to be or become	violate, tolerate, exacerbate, emanate
-en	to cause to be or have; to come to be or have	quicken, lengthen, frighten
-ify, -fy	to make, form into	beautify, electrify, rectify
-ize	to cause to be or become; to bring about	colonize, plagiarize, synchronize

WORD ROOTS

The following table lists the most common word roots, their meanings, and several examples of words with those roots. Whenever possible, the examples include both common words that are already part of your everyday vocabulary and words form the lessons in this book.

There are over 150 roots here, but don't be intimidated by the length of this list. Break it down into manageable chunks of 10–20 roots and memorize them section by section. Remember that you use words with these roots every day.

ROOT	MEANING	EXAMPLES
ac, acr	sharp, bitter	acid, acute, acrimonious
act, ag	to do, to drive, to force, to lead	agent, enact, agitate
ad, al	to, toward, near	adjacent, adhere, allure
al, ali, alter	other, another	alternative, alias, alien
am	love	amiable, amity, enamor
amb	to go, to walk	ambulatory, preamble, ambush
amb, amph	both, more than one, around	ambiguous, ambivalent, amphitheater
anim	life, mind, soul, spirit	unanimous, animosity equanimity
annui, ennui	year	annual, anniversary, perennial
anthro, andr	man, human	anthropology, android, misanthrope
apo	away	apology, apocalypse, apotheosis
apt, ept	skill, fitness, ability	adapt, adept, inept
arch, archi, archy	chief, principal, ruler	hierarchy, monarchy, anarchy
auto	self	automatic, autonomy, automaton
be	to be, to have a certain quality	befriend, bemoan, belittle
bel, bell	war	rebel, belligerent, antebellum
ben, bon	good	benefit, benevolent, bonus
cad, cid	to fall, to happen by chance	accident, coincidence, cascade
cant, cent, chant	to sing	chant, enchant, recant
cap, capit, cipit	head, headlong	capital, principal, capitulate
cap, cip, cept	to take, to get	capture, intercept, emancipate
card, cord, cour	heart	encourage, cardiac, discord
carn	flesh	carnivore, reincarnation, carnage
cast, chast	cut	caste, chastise, castigate
ced, ceed, cess	to go, to yield, to stop	exceed, concede, incessant
centr	center	central, concentric, eccentric
cern, cert, cret, crim, crit	to separate, to judge, to distinguish, to decide	ascertain, critique, discern
chron	time	chronic, chronology, synchronize
cis	to cut	scissors, precise, incisive
cla, clo, clu	shut, close	closet, enclose, preclude
claim, clam	to shout, to cry out	exclaim, proclaim, clamor
cli, clin	to lean toward, bend	decline, recline, proclivity
cour, cur	running, a course	recur, incursion, cursory
crat, cracy	to govern	democracy, autocracy, bureaucracy
cre, cresc, cret	to grow	creation, increase, increment
cred	to believe, to trust	incredible, credit, incredulous
cryp	hidden	crypt, cryptic, cryptography
cub, cumb	to lie down	succumb, incubate, incumbent
culp	blame	culprit, culpable, exculpate

ROOT	MEANING	EXAMPLES
dac, doc	to teach	doctor, indoctrinate, docile
dem	people	democracy, epidemic, pandemic
di, dia	apart, through	dialogue, diatribe, dichotomy
dic, dict, dit	to say, to tell, to use words	predict, dictionary, indict
dign	worth	dignity, indignant, disdain
dog, dox	opinion	dogma, orthodox, paradox
dol	suffer, pain	condolence, indolence, dolorous
don, dot, dow	to give	donate, endow, endow
dub	doubt	dubious, indubitable, dubiety
duc, duct	to lead	conduct, induct, conducive
dur	hard	endure, durable, obdurate
dys	faulty, abnormal	dysfunctional, dystopia, dyslexia
epi	upon	epidemic, epigram, epigraph
equ	equal, even	equation, equanimity, equivocate
err	to wander	err, error, erratic
esce	becoming	adolescent, coalesce, acquiesce
eu	good, well	euphoria, eulogy, euthanasia
fab, fam	speak	fable, famous, affable
fac, fic, fig, fait, feit, fy	to do, to make	fiction, factory, feign
fer	to bring, to carry, to bear	offer, transfer, proliferate
ferv	to boil, to bubble	fervor, fervid, effervescent
fid	faith, trust	confide, fidelity, infidel
fin	end	final, finite, affinity
flag, flam	to burn	flame, flammable, inflammatory
flect, flex	to bend	deflect, reflect, flexible
flu, flux	to flow	fluid, fluctuation, superfluous
fore	before	foresight, forestall, forbear
fort	chance	fortune, fortunate, fortuitous
fra, frac, frag, fring	to break	fracture, fraction, infringe
fus	to pour	confuse, infusion, diffuse
gen	birth, creation, race, kind	generous, genetics, homogenous
gn, gno	to know	ignore, recognize, incognito
grad, gress	to step	progress, aggressive, digress
grat	pleasing	grateful, gratitude, ingratiate
her, hes	to stick	cohere, adherent, inherent
(h)etero	different, other	heterosexual, heterogeneous, heterodox
(h)om	same	homogeneous, homonym, anomaly
hyper	over, excessive	hyperactive, hyperextend, hyperbole

ROOT	MEANING	EXAMPLES
id	one's own	idiom, idiosyncrasy, ideology
ject	to throw, to throw down	eject, dejected, conjecture
join, junct	to meet, to join	joint, junction, juxtapose
jur	to swear	jury, perjury, abjure
lect, leg	to select, to choose	election, select, eclectic
lev	lift, light, rise	elevator, lever, alleviate
loc, log, loqu	word, speech	dialogue, eloquent, loquacious
luc, lum, lus	light	illustrate, lucid, luminous
lud, lus	to play	illusion, elude, allude
lug, lut, luv	to wash	lavatory, dilute, deluge
mag, maj, max	big	magnify, magnitude, magnanimous
man	hand	manual, manufacture, manifest
min	small	minute, diminish, minutiae
min	to project, to hang over	prominent, imminent, preeminent
mis, mit	to send	transmit, remit, intermittent
mon, monit	to warn	monitor, admonish, remonstrate
morph	shape	amorphous, metamorphosis, anthropomorphic
mort	death	immortal, morbid, moratorium
mut	change	mutate, immutable, permutation
nam, nom, noun, nown, nym	rule, order	economy, taxonomy, autonomy
nat, nas, nai	to be born	native, nascent, renaissance
nec, nic, noc, nox	harm, death	innocent, noxious, innocuous
nom, nym, noun, nown	name	nominate, homonym, nominal
nounc, nunc	to announce	announce, pronounce, denounce
nov, neo, nou	new	novice, novel, neophyte
ob, oc, of, op	toward, to, against, completely, over	object, obstruct, obsequious
omni	all	omnipresent, omnipotent, omniscient
pac, peas	peace	pacify, appease, pacifier
pan	all, everyone	panorama, pandemic, panacea
par	equal	par, disparate, parity
para	next to, beside	parallel, paragon, paradox
pas, pat, path	feeling, suffering, disease	passionate, antipathy, apathetic
pau, po, pov, pu	few, little, poor	poverty, pauper, impoverish
ped	child, education	pediatrician, encyclopedia, pedantic
ped, pod	foot	pedestrian, expedite, impede
pen, pun	to pay, to compensate	penalty, punishment, penance
pend, pens	to hang, to weigh, to pay	depend, compensate, pensive

ROOT	MEANING	EXAMPLES
per	completely, wrong	perplex, permeate, pervade
peri	around	perimeter, peripheral, peripatetic
pet, pit	to go, to seek, to strive	compete, petition, impetuous
phil	love	philosophy, philanthropy, bibliophile
phone	sound	telephone, homophone, cacophony
plac	to please	placid, placebo, complacent
ple	to fill	complete, deplete, plethora
plex, plic, ply	to fold, to twist, to tangle, to bend	complex, comply, implicit
pon, pos, pound	to put, to place	expose, component, juxtapose
port	to carry	import, portable, importune
prehend, prise	to take, to get, to seize	surprise, apprehend, reprisal
pro	much, for, a lot	proliferate, profuse, proselytize
prob	to prove, to test	probe, probation, reprobate
pug	to fight	repugnant, pugnacious, impugn
punc, pung, poign	to point, to prick	point, puncture, punctilious
que, quis	to seek	inquisitive, conquest, query
qui	quiet	quiet, tranquil, acquiesce
rid, ris	to laugh	riddle, ridiculous, derision
rog	to ask	interrogate, surrogate, abrogate
sacr, sanct, secr	sacred	sacred, sacrament, sanction
sal, sil, sault, sult	to leap, to jump	assault, insolent, desultory
sci	to know	conscious, science, omniscient
scribe, scrip	to write	scribble, prescribe, circumscribe
se	apart	separate, segregate, seditious
sec, sequ	to follow	consequence, sequel, obsequious
sed, sess, sid	to sit, to be still, to plan, to plot	subside, assiduous, dissident
sens, sent	to feel, to be aware	sense, sentiment, dissent
sol	to loosen, to free	dissolve, resolution, dissolution
spec, spic, spit	to look, to see	perspective, speculation, circumspect
sta, sti	to stand, to be in place	static, obstinate, steadfast
sua	smooth	suave, persuade, dissuade
tac, tic	to be silent	tacit, reticent, taciturn
tain, ten, tent, tin	to hold	detain, sustain, tenacious
tend, tens, tent, tenu	to stretch, to thin	extend, tension, tenuous
theo	god	atheist, theology, apotheosis
tract	to drag, to pull, to draw	attract, detract, tractable
us, ut	to use	abuse, utility, usurp
ven, vent	to come, to move toward	convene, venture, intervene

ROOT	MEANING	EXAMPLES
er	truth	verdict, verisimilitude, veritable
vers, vert	to turn	revert, aversion, versatile
vi	life	vivid, vigorous, vicarious
vid, vis	to see	evident, survey, visionary
voc, vok	to call	vocal, advocate, equivocate
vol	to wish	volunteer, volition, benevolence

APPENDIX B

Additional Resources

This book has given you focused practice and review of your vocabulary skills. If you need more practice, these resources offer good places to find what you need to pass your test.

BOOKS

1001 Vocabulary and Spelling Questions, 2nd edition (New York: Learning Express, 2003).

501 Vocabulary Questions (New York: LearningExpress, 2003).

Bromberg, Murray, and Melvin Gordon. *1100 Words You Need to Know* (Hauppauge, NY: Barrons Educational Series, 2000).

Bryson, Bill. *Bryson's Dictionary of Troublesome Words* (New York: Broadway Books, 2002).

Elster, Charles. *Verbal Advantage: 10 Steps to an Impressive Vocabulary* (New York: Random House, 2000).

Merriam-Webster's Vocabulary Builder (Springfield: Merriam-Webster, 1999).

The Oxford Essential Dictionary of Difficult Words (New York: Oxford University Press, 2001).

Rozakis, Laurie. *Vocabulary for Dummies* (New York: Wiley, 2001).

Schneider, Meg. *Word Power* (New York: Kaplan, 2001).

Vocabulary and Spelling Success in 20 Minutes a Day, 3rd edition (New York: LearningExpress, 2002).

GENERAL WEBSITES

Vocabulary University. "Vocabulary"—**www.vocabulary.com:** vocabulary puzzles and exercises with words ranging from junior high to college level.

Edhelper.com. "Vocabulary"—**www.edhelper.com/vocabulary.htm:** vocabulary lessons and worksheets for grades 1–12.

www.freevocabulary.com: a list of 5,000 vocabulary words at the high school and college level.

Darling, Charles; Capital Community College. "Building a Better Vocabular."—**webster.commnet.edu/grammar/vocabulary.htm:** tips for building vocabulary and quizzes for over 350 words.

Schmidel, Dyann. "Quiz Hub: SAT Vocabulary Word Quiz"—**quizhub.com/quiz/f-vocabulary.cfm:** quizzes for selected SAT words.

Merriam-Webster, Inc. "Merriam-Webster's Vocabulary Builder"—**www.m-w.com/info/vocab/vocab.htm:** Greek and Latin word roots and quizzes; links to other vocabulary-building sites.

WORD OF THE DAY WEBSITES

"My Word A Day"—**www.mywordaday.com.**

Lexico Publishing Group. "Dictionary.com Word of the Day"—**http://dictionary.reference.com/wordoftheday/.**

Oxford University Press. "Oxford English Dictionary Word of the Day"—**http://oed.com/cgi/display/wotd.**

The New York Times Company. "Word of the Day"—**www.nytimes.com/learning/students/wordofday/.**

Wordsmith.org. "A Word A Day"—**www.wordsmith.org/awad.**